The New Challenge of

Secretary-General
Nikai Toshihiro

Morita Minoru

RONSO-SHA

Foreword—Nikai's challenge for lasting peace and the resilience of the global civilization

The new challenge of Secretary-General Nikai Toshihiro, who, with his international and world-historical view, has lived up to the belief that "It is me who bear difficulties" and acted as a "sincere No.2 statesman", for the world peace and the resilience of the global civilization

"It is the duty of government to make it difficult for people to do wrong, easy to do right" Gladstone

The origin of Nikai Toshihiro's politics is pacifism and love for his home, and he continues his challenge for the resilience of the global civilization with keeping these fundamental ideals.

What Covid-19 catastrophe poses to humankind is the fact that the global civilization is weakening. We humankind must put effort into the resilience of it. The next challenge of Secretary-General Nikai Toshihiro, who put the policy of national resilience at the center of Japanese politics, is the resilience of the global civilization. And he will boldly tackle with it, which is as important as national resilience. It is also a proof that Nikai is a true international politician.

Secretary-General Nikai, a politician of peace, benevolence, and tolerance, who is tackling the Covid-19 crisis, has taken on endless challenges to make a comfortable and safe society in which everyone can live comfortably. Nikai is one of those politicians with an international view, which has been rare in the history of Japan. And in this sense, he resembles Katsu Kaishu, who were active in the end days of Edo era and in the period of Meiji Restoration.

Furthermore, Nikai is also one of those rare politicians in that he, though domestically a No.2 figure, has acted for a long time as a politician who is more powerful than No.1 politicians.

Now, Nikai has been breaking the record of tenure as the Secretary-General of LDP, and here I quote an article from 'Jiyuu-Shimpoo' which covered it.

On September 8th 2020, 1,498 days have passed since Nikai Toshihiro became the Secretary-General of LDP, thus he broke the record by the former Prime Minister Tanaka Kakuei, whom Nikai admires as his "political mentor". As for the successive tenure as well, Nikai had already broken the record by Maeo Shigesaburo, a former chairman of the Lower House, so Nikai made a new record of both total and successive tenure. ('Jiyuu-Shimpoo' September 22nd 2020 edition)

The article continues as follows,

On the same day, asked about this record by the reporters, Nikai answered, "It is a result of making efforts steadily every day. I have never thought of breaking someone's records."

And about the future operation of LDP, it reports,

(Nikai) said, "A political party is responsible for promoting and checking the policies and plans by the government" and emphasized, "LDP is a party that has been constructed and protected by our great senior fellows and party members. So I will face the voices and feelings of the members steadily, humbly, and sincerely".

Secretary-General Nikai is just humble and has lived up to his conviction "I will bear the difficulties, and achievements are for others". "Achievements are for others, and I will always work in the background"—it is a way of life which politicians should live and Nikai is practicing this. All politicians must have this attitude of Nikai as their model.

In the "Record of Utterances" corner of 'Jiyuu-Shimpo' September 22nd 2020 issue, the comment by Nikai is recorded with the title "About the new record of tenure as the Secretary-General of LDP".

When evening comes every day, I feel that the day is over and I have to work diligently tomorrow. Though I broke the record, I have never thought of reaching or breaking someone's record. When asked about my new record, I just thought "Ah, is that so?".

Then, Nikai continued,

The national and admirable party organization of ours today, which has been constructed by our senior fellows, are made from many party members, as well as our branches formed from them. As you know, it cannot be made overnight. In this sense, we have to face it humbly and sincerely again.

It is by no means an easy task to act as a Secretary-General of Liberal Democratic Party for a long time; any politician who is to act as a Secretary-General for a long time must be a great and powerful figure. Acting as a Secretary-General is a daunting task. However, Nikai has achieved it and, as of May 2021, maintains this position.

Though the office term of the LDP president is three years, that of party officials is one year. And although the final decision on the appointment of party officials is made by the General Affairs Council, it would decide "entrusting on the president" and the officials are appointed by LDP president. Due to such a process, it is extremely difficult to remain as a Secretary-General, the central post among party officials, for a long time.

It is also difficult to remain as a LDP president, so a long-time administration like the previous Abe Cabinet is a rare case. Usually, when a LDP president changes, the Secretary-General changes as well. Thus it is a kind of miracle that Secretary-General Nikai remained in this position for more than 100 days even after the Abe Shinzo Cabinet ended and the Suga Yoshihide Cabinet started. It is because he is trusted by the former Prime Minister Abe, most of the LDP Diet members and its party members. Furthermore, it is because Nikai is a figure with outstanding political abilities and no one can replace him.

Even when the Prime Minister and LDP president changed, Nikai has continued to act as the Secretary-General. Suga Yoshihide, who became the new Prime Minister and LDP president, asked Nikai to remain in the position of Secretary-General, and he accepted it. Suga has inherited the Abe administration and the biggest inheritance is for Nikai to stay in office; it is another example of miracle.

There are various reasons for this miracle, and the biggest one is Nikai's political attitude in which he has acted up to sincerity, justice, and fairness, his outstanding political ability, and his way of life in which he has kept caring for others. And on top of that, one can point out the gifted political sense of him.

In my previous work, I listed Katsu Kaisyu, Suzuki Kantaro, Miki Bukichi, Tanaka Kakuei, and Nikai Toshihiro as genius politicians of the post-Edo era, and I believe that there are five characteristics which they had in common.

First, these geniuses mastered "art"—outstanding "art"—which Bismarck, the genius statesman of 19th century Germany, referred to in his saying "Politics is not science; it is art". These five geniuses know it.

Second, they are all hard worker as in the remark by Edison, the genius inventor, "Genius is one percent inspiration and ninety-nine percent perspiration". At the same time, they have "inspiration", which is required of any genius in any area.

Third, they are all geniuses of reading someone's mind; they have special faculty to read it. They had an ability to sense the true thoughts and feelings of people and could read the minds of their political rivals and negotiating partners.

Fourth, they all have "endless kindheartedness" toward ordinary people.

Fifth, they all made political decisions with the international viewpoint based on the world history.

Nikai is equipped with these five elements of "art", "inspiration", "faculty to read someone's mind", "kindheartedness", and "viewpoint based on the world history". More accurately, he has equipped himself with them through his long-time and earnest political activities and polished them

The biggest reason why I place high expectations on Nikai is, firstly, the fact that he is a hard-core pacifist; he has always acted up to pacifism. It is "protecting peace" that is the most important thing for humankind as well as politics.

Nikai values peaceful and friendly relations with neighboring Asian countries such as China and South Korea and has been saying, "A nation cannot move out, so we should be friendly with neighboring countries". I have accompanied Nikai on his visits to neighboring Asian countries many times and seen the reality of his friendship and goodwill activities firsthand. For Japan to exist peacefully, we have to maintain and develop peaceful and friendly relations with neighboring countries, and it is essential to achieve true world peace. Nikai has always made efforts to maintain such relationship, and it is the biggest reason why I place high expectations on him.

Another reason is the fact that Nikai, from the international point of view, has promoted the "disaster-prevention, disaster-reduction, and national resilience policy" and led the initiative for establishing "World Tsunami Awareness Day/November 5th" in U.N. And now, he is promoting the resilience of the whole human society in this Covid-19 crisis. We must make efforts to stabilize the human society through the resilience of both hardware and software. Furthermore, I believe that the idea of "resilience" should be extended to the "resilience of the global civilization", not just that of infrastructure, and Nikai will work on the "resilience of the human society" from the viewpoint based on the world history.

Nikai is not only a stalwart humanitarian but also a politician of "virtue" who loves ordinary people; he always turns his attention to the unfortunate people. There is a phrase by Laozi, " 上善若水 " (The highest virtue is like water. It always flows downstream and enriches there, then brings benefits to the whole), and Nikai practices politics based on it.

The political activities by Tanaka Kakuei, the mentor of Nikai, were based on the realization of the world peace and the "kindheartedness" toward every person, and Nikai inherits from Tanaka this basic spirit of "kindness".

The purpose of this work is to let the whole nation know "Secretary-General Nikai Toshihiro's new challenges for the resilience of the global civilization"—the challenges Reiwa Japan faces and the idea and vision of Secretary-General Nikai Toshihiro who aims for the perpetual peace and the resilience of the human society on the basis of the international and world-historical viewpoint.

I have published a lot of biographies of politicians and records of their activities. As for Nikai, I have just published "An Essay on Secretary-General Nikai Toshihiro" (Ronso-sha) on April 2020, but here I present this work soon after the previous work was published. It is because new challenges for Nikai's politics have emerged amid the drastic changes of the age. It would be extremely rare that one publishes two works on the same politician in such a short period, but it can be called a bond between Nikai and me. The more I learn about Nikai, the more strongly I feel the greatness of Nikai as a politician. The image of Nikai which I describe in these two works might be like describing mere several trees in a colossal jungle. I have written these works feeling sorry for him. Following my previous work, I will present to the readers how Nikai is going to create the new age of Reiwa Japan, how he is going to contribute to the history of humankind, and his true image, ideas, and activities.

I named this work "The New Challenge of Secretary-General Nikai Toshihiro" because the period of the "denouement of Nikai's politics" has begun in which Nikai challenges to the new age by his determination for lasting peace, which he has created in his long-time political activities, political wisdom and knowledge, political "inspiration", political art, genius faculty to read someone's mind, strong sense of justice, ethical ability, and his entire wisdom and ability by which he considers the future of entire humankind and acts with the international viewpoint based on the world history.

Nikai is a hard-core pacifist and at the same time has strong love for his home; he has always been regarding Wakayama as the origin of his politics and discussing with the people there. Thus, pacifism and love for his home are the starting point of Nikai Toshihiro as a politician.

Now, the world is in the midst of a tempestuous period.

The tension between U.S. and China is intensifying and nations around the world are pressed to choose which country they ally with. Furthermore, the world has begun to split around the rivalry between U.S. and China.

In the past, Japan has depended on the Japan-U.S. alliance for its security, while it has cooperated with China in economic matters. However, the U.S. government presses the Japanese government to value the Japan-U.S. alliance. But it is dangerous for Japan to come into collision with China. Japan relies on its economic prosperity, so it will face a crisis if its economy breaks down.

For Japan, there is no other way than to perform mediating diplomatic activities to pursue the reconciliation between U.S. and China and to seek to survive in the midst of the tension between these two countries.

It is Nikai who has the power to perform such mediating diplomatic activities; he is the only Japanese politician who can talk with Xi Jinping, President of China, in person.

Nikai plans to visit U.S. first so that he can take the first step for the reconciliation between U.S. and China when he visits China later.

I believe that Nikai has the courage to tackle with the historical issue of the reconciliation between U.S. and China.

Nikai has declared his intention to visit North Korea and he means it.

Nikai always performs his tasks with the intention of sacrificing himself.

Now, nothing is more important for humankind than to defend the world peace, and Nikai is going tackle with this great undertaking. I wait it in anticipation.

May 2021

Author

CONTENTS

Chapter 3　Nikai's outstanding political ability with which he exerted his keen intuition to realize the "100,000 yen benefit to every citizen" at the last moment, save people's lives and assure the people

Chapter 4　The true image of Secretary-General Nikai described by his closest aides—The origin of his genius political "intuition", his way of human diplomacy, deep love for his home Wakayama and great contribution to it, and "Nikai-ism" in which he has always dedicated himself for others

Chapter 5   A challenge for new issues—For eternal peace and the resilience of human society

Chapter 1

Nikai's exceptional skill by which he accomplished the smooth change of power, became the father of the Suga administration, and at the same time strengthened the solidarity of LDP, without creating a political vacuum despite the sudden resignation of former Prime Minister Abe

"It is man who does politics"—Confucius

1. Resignation of Prime Ministers and selection of their successors in the post-war political history

At the end of August 2020, Abe Shinzo, the former Prime Minister, suddenly resigned due to illness. It had been unexpected, but thanks to the political skill of Nikai Toshihiro, the Secretary-General of LDP, the selection of his successor and the change of power were accomplished smoothly without causing any confusion.

Here, let us look back those Prime Ministers who resigned due to illness after the World War II.

After World War II, the first Prime Minister who resigned due to illness was Ishibashi Tanzan. He was elected the president of LDP at the end of 1956 and became Prime Minister, but on January 1957, he determined to resign due to illness. His successor was Kishi Nobusuke, who was the Foreign Minister of the Ishibashi Cabinet.

This transition of power from the Ishibashi administration to the Kishi administration was a turning point of the course of Japan. While Ishibashi valued Asia, Kishi emphasized the relationship with U.S. Ishibashi appointed Kishi as the acting Prime Minister and LDP president, and the Kishi Cabinet was formed one month later.

The relationship between Ishibashi and GHQ was not so amicable. When Yoshida Shigeru was nominated as the Prime Minister and formed his cabinet in 1946, he appointed Ishibashi, who had been known for his strong mental power, as the Minister of Finance. Ishibashi focused on the measures against unemployment, and actively employed the returnees from former colonies of Japan and military veterans as well as the unemployed in central and local government-owned companies and paid them salary. He munificently spent the government funds which were deposited in the Ministry of Finance.

GHQ pressed Ishibashi to hand over the finances of Japanese government, but he refused it. Thus, GHQ developed a feeling of distrust against him and ousted him from public office; GHQ obtained the funds of Japanese government by expelling Ishibashi.

Meanwhile, Kishi skillfully made contact with GHQ when he was incarcerated in Sugamo Prison as a Class-A war criminal and accomplished the release of himself. On the other hand, GHQ used the influence of Kishi, the leader of people who had been engaged in the operation of former Manchuria, to control Japan. As a result, for GHQ, Ishibashi and Kishi were their enemy and friend respectively.

When Ishibashi resigned due to illness, pro-U.S. Kishi came in. Later, when I met with Kishi, he said in a matter-of-fact way, "It was all fortune. I believe my chance never came if Mr. Ishibashi didn't get ill".

The second Prime Minister who resigned due to illness was Ikeda Hayato, who resigned on October 1964 and appointed Sato Eisaku as his successor.

The third was Ohira Masayoshi, who passed away on June 1980 as the incumbent Prime Minister. His successor, Suzuki Zenko, formed his cabinet thirty-six days later.

The fourth was Obuchi Keizo, who resigned due to sudden illness on April 2000. And this time, his successor, Mori Yoshiro, formed his cabinet as early as the next day.

The fifth was Abe Shinzo, who resigned on September 2007; Fukuda Yasuo, the successor, formed his cabinet sixteen days later.

The sixth was also Abe Shinzo, who again resigned due to illness at the end of August 2020 and was succeeded by Suga Yoshihide; the Suga Cabinet was formed twenty days after the announcement of Abe's resignation.

These resignations due to illness and appointments of successors were all performed quite quickly; the shortest was the shift from the Obuchi Cabinet to the Mori Cabinet, and the longest was the one from the Ohira Cabinet to the Suzuki Cabinet. The reason why the latter took so long time was the fact that Miyazawa Kiichi and Ito Masayoshi, who had been asked to become the next Prime Minister, declined it. In this way, Suzuki Zenko got a chance to become the new Prime Minister.

However, there is one significant difference between the change of power in 2020 and those in the past. Before, any Prime Minister who resigned due to illness never appeared in front of the people in good health. Though Prime Minister Ishibashi regained health after resignation, it took relatively long time. And Prime Minister Abe (in his first cabinet) came back after some period of rehabilitation. Abe is the only Prime Minister who got this position again after resigning due to illness, but it took five years.

In 2020, though Prime Minister Abe resigned due to illness again, he acted as Prime Minister until his successor, Suga Yoshihide, assumed this position. Even after the Suga Cabinet was formed, Abe has been engaging in political activities as a Diet member just the same as when he was healthy. Furthermore, some in the political circle talked about his third resurgence and, because he seemed so healthy, wondered whether he had been actually ill or not. However, as the issue of political funds of Abe's office around "A party to appreciate cherry blossom" was subjected to the investigation by the prosecution, a rumor about Abe becoming the Prime Minister and LDP president for the third time is disappearing, and many considers Abe's political life has ended. Thus, Prime Minister Suga got a chance to become independent from his predecessor Abe. We should look carefully how Suga uses this chance.

Those Prime Ministers mentioned above didn't appear in front of the people in good health, except Abe.

In the past, the handover of power was done quickly, but at the same time forcefully, so it typically left bad feeling within the party. But the handover of power from Abe to Suga, which was done on August and September 2020, didn't left significant complaint, distrust, trouble, or bad feeling, because it was performed smoothly according to the party rules.

It was thanks to the skillful management of the party by Secretary-

General Nikai Toshihiro, who had been entrusted by Abe everything about the handover of power, that the transition of government was finished smoothly.

Although some complained that the voting by all party members was omitted, the measures by Nikai were in line with the rule of the party, so such complaints subsided soon. In other words, the concern of the party members about Covid-19 catastrophe and the political vacuum outweighed those complaints. Therefore, most of them accepted Nikai's measures.

For those who demanded the voting by the party members, each Prefectural branch provided the chance of preliminary election, and its result was adopted as the principle of the Prefectural branch in the LDP presidential election. In my view, the complaints among local organizations and ordinary party members were almost resolved.

Nikai's measures during the transition of government in 2020 succeeded in the end, and the biggest reason for it was his leadership ability which had been highly matured. Also, his quick actions contributed to the success as well. During the change of power from Abe to Suga, Nikai, who had been entrusted everything by Abe, played a significant role.

The media focused exclusively on the point that Nikai led the formation of the Suga Cabinet, but it is nothing more than one of his many accomplishments.

The most outstanding accomplishment of Nikai is that he managed the party fairly and processed the matters in a way that they caused no complaints or bad feeling; LDP's unity was maintained.

Nikai acted aggressively so that Suga could become the LDP president and Prime Minister because he had decided that in order to minimize the confusion within the ruling party caused by the sudden resignation of Abe, Suga, who was the former chief Cabinet secretary and had managed the government along with Prime Minister Abe, would be the best choice. Thanks to Nikai's decision, the confusion could be avoided.

After the election of LDP president, Ishiba Shigeru, who was third in the election, and the officials of Ishiba faction made almost no complaints. Ishiba took responsibility for the loss and resigned the chief of Ishiba faction (Suigetsu-kai), and I felt this proved his sincerity and seriousness. Ishiba faction continued to exist under the collective executive system, and Tamura Norihisa, who is a Lower House member and the secretary-general of Ishiba faction, was appointed the Minister of Health, Labour, and Welfare of the Suga Cabinet. Thus, the unity within the party could be maintained.

Similarly, complaints from Kishida Fumio, who was second in the LDP presidential election, and the members of Kishida faction weren't heard so much. Among the members of Kishida faction, Hirai Takuya and Kawakami Yoko joined the cabinet and the whole-party approach was maintained. Kishida is acting for the next chance.

The transition from the Abe administration to the Suga administration proceeded both peacefully and smoothly and left almost no bad feeling. It was due to the excellent skill of Nikai, who resolved to minimize the political vacuum and confusion, and I believe it should be valued as an accomplishment of him. Some media has been trying to form a network for restraining the enormous power of Nikai, but I say they are stupid.

What is important is the whole-party approach and cooperation of the entire party. And Nikai is making efforts to defend the party unity day and night.

2. The twenty days of the Japanese political circles to which the whole world paid attention (From August 28th to September 16th)

The news of Abe's resignation stunned the world because it was so sudden.

Here, I look back the situation since the resignation of Abe until the formation of the Suga Cabinet.

On August 28th, Prime Minister Abe held a press conference in the office of the Prime Minister and announced his resignation. At the same time, he entrusted everything regarding the matters after his resignation to Secretary-General Nikai.

LDP held a special meeting by its officials and confirmed that such matters as the method and the date of the election which choose the successor of Abe would be entrusted to Secretary-General Nikai and that specific procedures would be made in the General Affairs Council held on September 1st.

About the LDP presidential election, Nikai said, "if party members consider it necessary due to urgent situation etc., I will take emergent measures", and declared his intention to "hold the presidential election in a general assembly of its Diet members, instead of a general assembly of party members, if situation requires".

On August 29th, Nikai Toshiro, the Secretary General of LDP, and Suga Yoshihide, the chief Cabinet secretary, held a talk.

And this day, in a room of the public dormitory for Lower House members, Suga, Nikai, Hayashi Motoo, the Acting Secretary-General, and Moriyama Hiroshi, the Diet Affairs Committee chief, held a talk. And it was reported in the media that Suga declared his intention to run for the presidential election.

On August 30th, Suga said, "I will focus on the measures against Covid-19 and for the economy". In LDP, this talk was regarded as his declaration to run for the presidential election.

In the morning of September 1st, the General Affairs Council was held, and it was decided that the presidential election which would choose the successor of Abe be held in a general assembly of LDP Diet members, instead of a nationwide vote by the party members. About choosing the new president through a vote by only its Diet members and representatives of prefectures, Nikai said, "we have to establish the new administration as soon as possible. It is emergent and I would ask the election in a general assembly of Diet members".

On September 2nd, Nikai faction (Shisuikai) handed a request to

Suga asking him to run for the presidential election. Though Nikai is the chairperson of his faction, he has entrusted its management to Kawamura Takeo, the acting chairperson. Thus, it was Kawamura who led the activities of Nikai faction.

On the same day, the chairpersons of Hosoda faction, Aso faction, and Takeshita faction held a press conference together and declared that they would support Suga. It helped to ensure that Suga would be chosen as the next LDP president.

On September 8th, in a press conference held in the LDP headquarters, Nikai took a cautious view toward an early Lower House dissolution and general election, making "early dissolution and general election on October 25th" less likely. He said that Lower House dissolution is up to a Prime Minister, adding, "currently, there are no issues for which we should ask for the judgment of the people, so we don't have to hurry. It is not a time to ask Prime Minister (for the dissolution)". Thus, he demanded junior Diet members to calm down, who had been influenced by the rumor of early dissolution, and it was natural for him to do so due to the Covid-19 catastrophe. Furthermore, about the appointment of the party officials and the formation of new cabinet, he said, "they were more important than any other issues, so the new president should think them over. Of course, I would support him if asked". In this way, Nikai showed his attitude to support Prime Minister.

On September 14th, the general assembly by LDP Diet members was held and Suga was elected as the new president of LDP.

Abe Shinzo, the former president, said, "I apologize for resigning before the end of my tenure. And I am thankful that the presidential election was held orderly with Secretary-General Nikai at the core". And the transition of power from Abe to Suga was performed smoothly.

Suga Yoshihide, the newly elected LDP president, referred to the name of Aso Taro, the Vice Prime Minister and Minister of Finance, and Nikai Toshihiro, the Secretary-General of LDP, and implied their reappointment, saying, "they are the core of the cabinet and the party, extremely important for the management of administration".

On September 15th, an interim General Affairs Council was held, and the new officials of the party were chosen. Nikai was reappointed, but the General Affairs Council chief, the Policy Affairs Research Council chief, and the Election Campaign Committee chief were replaced. When asked about an early dissolution of Diet, Nikai answered, "it is a matter the Prime Minister decides. It is a crucial political issue, so I would like to discuss with the new president Suga on a daily basis and make efforts to manage the party smoothly". In this way, he emphasized on the unity between the Prime Minister and Secretary-General.

At the same time, he called for the unity of the party as well, emphasizing, "We must never cause a squabble within the party. It is important to cooperate as one party, stimulate the party, and meet the expectations of the people".

On September 16th, Diet opened an extraordinary session, and both the Lower House and Upper House appointed Suga, the new president of LDP, as the ninety-ninth Prime Minister. On the next day, the Suga Cabinet was formed, and his administration began.

On September 17th, Secretary-General Nikai gave a speech at a fund-raising party of Ishiba faction and called for the unity within the party, saying, "We must unite under the new Prime Minister Suga and make the nation move forward". And he encouraged Ishiba, saying, "you are entrusted a task to take responsibility for the new age". At the same time, he emphasized the necessity of the friendly relationship with China.

On the same day, Nikai talked with Motegi Toshimitsu, the Foreign Minister and the acting chairperson of Takeshita faction, and discussed the political management in the future.

On September 18th, the extraordinary session for appointing the new Prime Minister was closed.

During these twenty days since the sudden resignation of the former Prime Minister Abe Shinzo, the world paid attention to the political movement in Japan, and the transition of power from the Abe administration to the Suga administration completed smoothly, without any confusion. A daunting task of the change of power was finished safely by the skillful party management of Secretary-General Nikai.

Nikai pierced through to Suga's intentions, drew forth them, and opened the way for selecting Suga as the new Prime Minister and LDP president. Though he had been devoting his entire attention to act as a No.2 figure of the Abe administration and denying the ambition to be the No.1 politician, he predicted precisely that Suga was willing to take over the reins of government. Again, it proved the fact that Nikai has an ability to read someone's mind.

Given the importance of the relationship with Komeito, the partner of the coalition, Nikai has kept constant contact with its top officials. The trustful relationship between Nikai and the leadership of Komeito is unshakable.

In addition, Nikai has made careful note of the appointment of the cabinet members and the officials of Diet and the party and made efforts to reduce dissatisfaction within the party. As for personnel issues, the careful attention of a leader is essential, and the frustration within LDP around personnel issues disappeared due to Nikai's careful attention.

By the end of September 2020, officials of Diet, vice ministers and parliamentary secretaries of the government, and officials of the party had been all selected and appointed, and there was no apparent complaint within LDP. Thus, it can be said that the personnel issue was processed peacefully and smoothly. I say again that it is greatly due to the outstanding political skill of Secretary-General Nikai.

While the Abe administration was called "Abe - Aso - Suga government" in LDP, now many call the Suga administration "Suga - Nikai government". Suga, the new Prime Minister, will make decision on important matters by discussing with Nikai. If the harmonious relationship between Prime Minister Suga and Secretary-General Nikai collapses, the Suga Cabinet will face a crisis. I believe both Suga and Nikai know it well.

3. Nikai always talks about politics with plain words

Nikai has always talked about politics with plain words and communicated political issues to each of the people. Following the formation of the new administration of Suga, Nikai told in an interview with "Jiyuu-Minsyu (October 20th 2020 Edition)", the party paper of LDP, about the Lower House election which would be held in a year and how they should proceed with the party activities as LDP. Because it is the party paper, he talked mainly to the party members, but I believe his words contain an important message for the ordinary people other than the party members, so here I quote the whole text of the interview.

Nikai is acting as the Secretary-General of LDP for a fifth term, which is the longest tenure in the history. And he has continued to lead the party management as the key person after the change of power from the Abe administration to the Suga administration. We asked Secretary-General Nikai about his determination for the Lower House general election which will be held in a year and his enthusiasm about getting more party members, the basis of the party.

— What do you aspire to do in your fifth term as Secretary-General?
Nikai: I will approach tasks with a fresh mind as in my first term and make efforts to manage the party smoothly. I renew my resolve "to do politics for the people" every day and devote myself on the party management.
— On October 16th, one month will have passed since the formation of the Suga Cabinet. How do you regard the progress up to now?
Nikai: I think it has made a good start for now. In the world of politics, vacuum is never allowed even in a moment. Thanks to the cooperation by the members and friends of the party, the presidential election was held smoothly and the Suga administration, which inherits the Abe administration, was formed. They are approaching tasks speedily with the slogan "the cabinet working for the people". Thus, we support them at full power and approach the task of building the nation which Prime Minister

Suga aims for together.

— This month, Diet will hold the extraordinary session as well.

Nikai: First of all, in this session, we have to convey clear messages from the ruling party on the issues the people are concerned about, such as measures against Covid-19.

It will not be easy to proceed with both preventing the spread of infection and encouraging economic activities, but in this session, we, with the close cooperation with Komeito, will devote ourselves to show the people that each issue is addressed steadily.

Meanwhile, are we prepared adequately for a series of natural disasters? I think that the expectation of the people for disaster-prevention, disaster-reduction, and national resilience is still strong. Therefore, in discussions in the Diet and in the 2021 budget draft at the end of this year, we hope to carry a powerful message that can relieve the people.

— The acquirement of new party members in 2020 will be closed at the year's end. How do you resolve for it?

Nikai: The party members and party friends are the basis of the party structure. I hope their day-to-day efforts increase the number of our fellows and achieve "one million and two thousand hundred party members".

We will be vigorously engaged in the campaign to acquire new party members, so I sincerely ask "the cooperation of everyone".

— The tenure of Lower House members will end in a year. How do you resolve for the general election?

Nikai: I have repeatedly said that we are always prepared in case the Diet is dissolved tomorrow, so I have an attitude of "always in the battlefield" for the next general election of the Lower House.

I will clearly show to the people the achievements of the Abe administration, which has accomplished political stability and resolved many issues during those seven years and eight months, and get support from them on the determination of the Suga administration to develop those achievements further.

The bond with the electorate cannot be achieved overnight. Each one of us must consciously approach with it in our day-to-day activities. And how much support the commitment of the candidates and branch chiefs will get from the electorate, and to what extent they will extend are important in the end. Laugh or cry we have only one year, so we will struggle nationwide and head for the victory together.

Nikai pointed out that the new Suga administration began smoothly and no political vacuum emerged, and clearly explained the measures against Covid-19 and the importance of the alliance with Komeito, its coalition partner. This kind of clarity and plainness is the true value of Secretary-General Nikai.

There is a saying "Full of courtesy, full of craft". It means that those who resort to blandishments and fawning smiles are apt to lack compassion, but Nikai in this interview was just the opposite and his words are sincere and with the spirit. Nikai is a politician of "A fortitude and unsophisticated person is almost compassionate" and has always lived the "Silence is gold" way of life. His words in this interview with "Jiyuu-Minsyu" were sincere and plain and cut straight the point. Thus, it can be regarded as an excellent message for the people.

When the fifth term as Secretary-General began, Nikai said as follows. He is just humble.

I have been given the important position as Secretary-General again. I will act with a fresh mind as in my first term, support the new party president Suga as the Secretary-General whose job is to take care of the party affairs, and make efforts to manage the party smoothly.

Our country now faces various challenges such as proceeding with the measures against the Covid-19 infection as well as social and economic activities in a compatible way, and tackling with the issue of successive natural disasters. Therefore, political vacuum is not allowed even in a moment. Our party will unite in supporting the Suga administration which, under the slogan of "the Cabinet which works for the people", continues the efforts of Mr. Abe, the former Prime Minister and party president, who has led the country with his extraordinary leadership, and is prepared to do the politics for the people.

The tenure of Lower House members ends in a year and a half, and I will tackle party activities with the attitude of "always in the battlefield". I sincerely ask the support of everyone, including the party members and party friends.

2021 is the year in which both the world and Japan face a great shift of a historical scale. The Covid-19 catastrophe, abnormal natural disasters, destabilization of the world situation, the world economic crisis and intensifying social conflict due to the increased social and economic gap are just a part of political challenges now. In such a situation, the Lower House election will be held, and it will be a time of trial for both Prime Minister Suga and Secretary-General Nikai. Therefore, the gifted political skill of Nikai must be exercised to the full extent. The future of not only the Suga administration but the coalition of LDP and Komeito depends on whether LDP can unite as one party under Nikai and exert its power.

While Nikai is at the core of the domestic politics of Japan, he always looks at the world.

Nikai is a politician of peace who has made efforts to accomplish the lasting peace of the world, and at the same time tackling with the resilience of the human society in order to protect the lives and assets of humankind against natural disasters and the Covid-19 infection.

The ideal of Nikai is to establish an international cooperation for the lasting peace and the resilience of human society, secure the Japanese people in it, and create a Japan respected by the international community in the peaceful environment.

Though Nikai is old, he is still so active.

Chapter 2

The ideal for action and the true image of Secretary-General Nikai Toshihiro—Nikai always talks with the spirit of Tanaka Kakuei, his political mentor, and keeps seeking for the peace and the happiness of the people

"To practice benevolence, you need utmost courage" ——*Gandhi*

1. Under the awareness "I am the inheritor of Tanaka Kakuei's politics", Nikai has been doing his political activities in which he has acted up to the love for the people

During the 1960s and the early 70s, I met with Tanaka Kakuei several times. Though most of my meetings with Tanaka were joint interviews, I could hear his talks from the very near distance. He was frank and natural, with great and good nature. Tanaka stepped into the political spotlight during the administrations of Kishi Nobusuke, Ikeda Hayato, and Sato Eisaku, and he became the Prime Minister after Sato.

In 1958, Tanaka was appointed the Minister of Posts and Telecommunications of the Kishi Cabinet, and in the period of the Ikeda Cabinet, he displayed his competent ability as the Policy Affairs Research Council chief of LDP. In LDP, the post of Policy Affairs Research Council chief has been so important, and it became so when Tanaka was in this position. In other words, he made Policy Affairs Research Council chief the most important role next to the Secretary-General.

After that, Tanaka acted as the Minister of Finance, the Secretary-General of LDP, and the Minister of International Trade and Industry, then became the Prime Minister in 1972. During this period, I heard Tanaka's talks in person, mainly in a joint interview by retired newspaper reporters. He was popular among the retired reporters and veteran reporters, and was intimate with the political commentators who had worked as political reporters. He was clean-cut and likable, and never arrogant or swaggering.

When Tanaka became the Prime Minister on July 1972, he was called the "Taiko (retired regent) of the present-day" and extremely popular. When the notion that only highly educated men could be a Prime Minister was dominant, the fact that a man who had graduated from only a higher elementary school became the Prime Minister gave big hopes to the people.

On September 1972, he flew to Beijing, talked with Zhou Enlai and Mao Zedong, and accomplished the establishment of diplomatic relations between Japan and China. And it made Tanaka more popular.

In my memory, it was the new year party held in the office of Prime Minister on January 4th 1974 that I came close to him and had the chance to talk with him in the near distance. He was voluble and made the listeners laugh often; he was just a nice person.

My impression about Tanaka Kakuei is that as he became a powerful figure in the political world, his expression changed and looked good. He was cheerful and straightforward without any distracting thoughts.

In 1972, shortly before Tanaka became the Prime Minister, an acquaintance of mine who worked at the Ministry of International Trade and Industry invited me to a study group on "The plan for remodeling the Japanese archipelago", so I participated in it. And when Tanaka was appointed the Prime Minister, his 'The plan for remodeling the Japanese archipelago' became a bestseller. Studying its contents, I, too, felt it was a good concept and decided to cooperate with it. Especially, the concept of the "simultaneous resolution of the excessive concentration in big cities and the depopulation of rural areas" seems excellent, so I wrote some critical essays from the standpoint of affirming Tanaka's concept, but they couldn't attract so much attention.

However, on October 1973, when Tanaka's politics went smoothly, Yom Kippur War broke out and a great shift occurred in the world politics: the oil crisis. The world and Japan suffered a substantial inflation, and it became impossible to promote the plan for remodeling the Japanese archipelago. Tanaka's aggressive economic policies failed. In the Upper House election held in the summer of 1973, LDP suffered a crushing defeat, and he was forced to resign in the autumn. At first, everyone had expected the Tanaka Cabinet to be powerful one, but the oil crisis crushed it.

After his resignation, Tanaka, who had already been in a mire politically, suffered the Lockheed bribery scandals plotted by the U.S. establishment and became the punching bag for the media. Furthermore, Miki Takeo, then the Prime Minister, used this plot and had the prosecutors arrest Tanaka, his political enemy. What Miki did totally contradicted the traditional way of conservative politics in which one should not drive in the corner even his political enemy, and it obviously crossed the line. In conservative politics, one must not treat his political enemy cruelly.

Afterwards, Tanaka continued to struggle to restore his honor, but he got ill and passed away as a defendant. The U.S. government and the political circles of Japan, which had subordinated itself to U.S., discarded a great statesman.

Meanwhile, I kept studying Tanaka Kakuei and contributing essays on him to general magazines. I not only felt deep sympathy for him but believed that the persecution of Tanaka by the U.S. establishment and the Miki Cabinet was unjust, so I continued to follow my own path among the media which was totally antagonistic against him.

At that time, I contributed to a general magazine every month, and many of my articles were about Tanaka. I visited Niigata prefecture dozens of times to study him and interview with the people in Niigata, especially the electorate in the Niigata No.3 constituency. I talked with even the wife of a farmer who worked in their field and listened to her story about Tanaka. Hearing from hundreds of people, I learned the depth of their love for Tanaka and his greatness.

Then, I got familiar with Hashimoto Tomisaburo, who acted as the Secretary-General of LDP in the early period of the Tanaka Cabinet, and Okuda Keiwa, a Lower House member and an aide of Tanaka. They were staunch and excellent politicians and supported me to report in LDP. Hashimoto faced prosecution in the Lockheed scandal and was unfortunate in the last stage of his life, but I was, and am, convinced that he was falsely charged. And to me, Okuda, five years older than me, was a great person and, for me, like an elder brother. He even invited me to his private gatherings. Hata Tsutomu, who would become the Prime Minister, was often with him. Hata, like Nikai, was straightforward and sincere person.

It was through Okuda that I got acquainted with Nikai. Okuda once told me that he had been instructed by Tanaka to support Nikai, who would run for the Diet election for the first time, as a top official of Tanaka faction. Tanaka paid attention to Nikai even before he became a Lower House member; Tanaka was aware of the excellent quality of Nikai as a politician. Okuda said, "It was remarkable that Tanaka Kakuei paid special attention on a freshman lawmaker beforehand". Tanaka might have detected Nikai's ability and potential as an excellent politician.

There is a phrase which I recall whenever I consider the relationship between Tanaka and Nikai. It is "A great genius is made by another great genius" by Heine, a great poet of Germany.

Tanaka was unfortunate in the last stage of his life, but it can be said that he bequeathed a genius politician, Nikai Toshihiro, for the Japan forty years later.

Tanaka loved the people of Japan, his home, and peace, and fought for the happiness of people and eliminating discrimination to the end. Nikai is just as the same and in this sense the inheritor of Tanaka's politics. The basis of Nikai's political activities is the same as that of Tanaka: peace, benevolence, and tolerance.

In 'Monthly Japan' (November 2020 issue), there is an interview with Nikai titled "How would Mr. Kakuei think now?" In this, Nikai said as follows.

"Mr. Tanaka was a great politician who was always gentle. He felt affection for people, especially those who were in unfortunate circumstances. I think it is wonderful. We served Mr. Tanaka with respect and felt that we could follow him to the end. And this feeling is just the same even now. When something happens, I have always stopped and thought, 'how would Mr. Tanaka think of it?'"

Tanaka valued rural areas, and so does Nikai. About this, Nikai told as follows.

"In politics, one must work out what kind of energy he should exercise for rural areas or developing regions. And LDP has tackled it for a long time. We want to make further efforts to energize those rural areas together with the local people. And their combined power will lead to the development of the national land. LDP will never abandon any regions."

Tanaka realized the re-establishment of diplomatic relations with China and valued Asia highly. He was a pacifist, and in this sense as well, Nikai is the inheritor of Tanaka's politics. Nikai said as follows.

"I believe Japan and China ... should cooperate mutually and act in the international community according to their ability and past performance. If Japan and China combine their power, we can take an important role in the international community, so both countries should make efforts and respond to the expectation from all over the world."

Nikai dedicates himself to the diplomatic activities initiated by the party as well. He said as follows.

"LDP itself should pursue diplomatic activities and lend a helping hand to the government. I, too, will visit foreign countries such as U.S. and China with my comrades at an appropriate time."

Nikai is determined to promote LDP's own diplomatic activities in order to supplement the governmental diplomacy. We should take notice of his party diplomatic activities and those initiated by Diet members.

2. Nikai knows well how to live politely

Those who get acquainted with Nikai would feel that he is too sincere a master of caring and a man of outstanding heart. In other words, he is a master of human relations; he is always sincere and kind. There is a book which has never left from my mind since I got familiar with Nikai. It is 'Caigentan', an excellent textbook about human relations. At the first, I thought that Nikai had learned from this book how to live admirably.

After World War II, many politicians and business executives read this book and learned what human relations mean. It is said that Tanaka Kakuei and Matsushita Konosuke read it, and many people read this book as a text for general culture.

'Caigentan' was written by Hong Zicheng of Ming Dynasty. This title was derived from a phrase by Wang Xinmin of Song Dynasty, "if you can chew vegetable roots you can accomplish anything." This means that if one lives simple life, is indifferent to material goods and comfortable even in poverty, he will be troubled by nothing. The author, Hong Zicheng, was well-versed in Confucianism, the thought of Laozi and Zhuangzi, and Buddhism.

Nikai is a person of extensive reading; I have accompanied him to a famous antiquarian bookshop in Kanda district, and he was a regular customer of it. I bought some books there as well, but Nikai bought several dozens of books. Furthermore, they covered broad areas such as history, culture, education and art. He is quite a bookish person, though he has never called himself so. In addition, he is well-versed in Chinese classic.

While many people might know what is written in Caigentan, few take these words as their own flesh and practice them. In fact, I am one of those people; I am precisely one of "those who read Analects but know nothing of them" and "those who read Caigentan but know nothing of them."

I felt Nikai had equipped himself with the words of Caigentan and been practicing them. However, it was just an assumption of mine and those who were close to Nikai told me that he had been a master of the art of managing in society even from his childhood and learned the perfect art of human relations in his youth.

Nikai's teachers of life were his parents. They were both persons of character and great figures who loved ordinary people and kept contributing to the development of the area. So Nikai learned from the great parents graceful manners in his childhood.

Here let us look the contents of Caigentan.

In Caigentan, there are some phrases which have been taught frequently in seminars for business executives etc. And I quote some of them (The text has been translated to modern language).

"In human relations, you must not show your feelings of likes and dislikes too much."

"One should be capacious enough to accept anybody, regardless of good or evil, wise or fool."

"Success always lies in struggles."

"Do not forget failure comes from your strong point."

"Those who reproach someone for his faults must know that all their words might become swords which hurt themselves."

"If he exerts the power of wealth, I will resist it by the virtue of human-heartedness, and if he exerts the power of honor, I will resist it by the righteous way."

"Even after the sun sets, the evening sky glows beautifully. Therefore, a wise man, in the last stage of his life, should stimulate his spirit and live an admirable life."

"Reduce your share of good foods to a third and give the rest to the other—Such deed is a way to live peacefully and happily."

"When one lives in this world, standing back a step will lead to the next step forward."

"You cannot get happiness by trying to do so. If you always live with joyous heart, happiness comes itself."

"You must tolerate mistakes of others, while you have to be unforgiving to your own errors. Endure your suffering, but do not ignore the suffering of others."

"Do not reproach others for their small mistakes, do not reveal their secrets, and forget their old wounds. If you follow these three rules in treating others, not only your personality improves but also you will never incur their hatred."

"When a member of your family makes mistake, do not bark at him or ignore it. You should expostulate with them with some reason. If it doesn't still work, you should warn him some time later."

"The master is personality, and talent is nothing more than a servant. If you are blessed with talent but not excellent personality, it is like a servant doing what he likes while his master is away. Then, the house will become a nexus for specters."

"If you put yourself in a circumstance where you don't have to be busy, you will not be upset a bit however the world thinks of you. If your mind is always quiet, you will not be distracted a bit however the world evaluates you."

"Even when you are beset from all sides, do not give up and escape from it."

"It is true that those who doesn't know tricks or bargains to frame up or deceive others are wise. However, those who know such tricks but can live without using them are actually the wisest."

"You would rather let little fishes hate you. It is much better than to be fawned by them. On the other hand, you should be scolded harshly by a person of character."

"You should forget the obligation someone owes to you, but do not forget the nuisance you gave him. Do not forget the obligation you owe to someone, but you should forget the hatred incurred by him."

"Those who can reflect on themselves straightforwardly are able to turn their every experience into the medicine to improve themselves. On the other hand, those who shift blame to others cannot improve a bit and will be a nobody."

These phrases in Caigentan, taught often in such places as seminars for business executives, are well-known, but few equip themselves with and practice them daily.

I thought that Nikai was called a master of life because he had equipped himself with and practice them in day-to-day life. However, my notion that Nikai had learned Caigentan well and been practicing them was just wrong. In fact, Nikai had practiced what was written in Caigentan long before he read the book.

Tsuruho Yosuke, who has always been with Nikai in various activities, said, "Mr. Nikai holds particular rules about the discipline of his deeds and practices them." Tsuruho is a comrade of Nikai who has held Nikai as his political mentor, so he knows about Nikai very well.

Nikai learned from his parents, who were called "saints" by surrounding people, and has practiced the moral discipline of deeds which he created by himself. And this discipline is almost the same as that in Caigentan. It is surprising and I believe Nikai is a genius in this sense.

3. Nikai is an exceptionally famous figure in China along with Tanaka Kakuei

Several years ago, I was invited by a friend of mine, a journalist who knew China well, to participate in a symposium on Japan-China relations held in Shangdong University and made a short speech there. Famous scholars of China, high officials of Chinese Communist Party, and military staffs were also present.

This symposium was held right after the DPJ (Democratic Party of Japan) administration led by Prime Minister Noda Yoshihiko ignored the protest by the Chinese government and forced through the nationalization of Senkaku Islands, intensifying the tension between Japan and China to the extreme. As a result, the interest in the relationship between Japan and China was very high, and those Chinese people paid attention to my words. Then, I was invited to several symposiums and asked to report the situation. In addition, I gave a lecture to the students of the graduation school of Shangdong University.

Just before leaving for China, I asked Nikai, who was widely known in China, to write a message, and when I presented it in a meeting, I was faced with questions about Nikai. Then, a Chinese staff told me a fact that most Chinese people knew the name of Nikai Toshihiro. And a scholar said, "The most famous Japanese in China are 'Tanaka Kakuei' and 'Nikai Toshihiro'". Hearing this, I keenly sensed that many Chinese people saw Tanaka and Nikai favorably.

Tanaka was the Prime Minister when the diplomatic relations between Japan and China was established in 1972, and Japanese and Chinese media repeatedly reported the talks with Mao Zedong and Zhou Enlai, the leaders of China then. As a result, Tanaka became the most famous figure in China.

Nikai is as famous as Tanaka in China. When I asked why so many Chinese people knew the name of Nikai Toshihiro well, the Chinese person answered, "Right after the 2008 Sichuan earthquake, Nikai quickly came to support us with a lot of relief material. He entered in dangerous areas wearing working cloth, visited the afflicted people, and encouraged them. And this was reported repeatedly all over China. Thus, Chinese people came to know the name of Mr. Nikai".

Chinese people say, "Mr. Nikai comes soon when we Chinese people suffer. In the past, when SARS spread in China, three Japanese politicians walked around Beijing and proved the city was safe". The three politicians were Yamasaki Taku (then the Secretary-General of LDP), Fuyushiba Tetsuzo (then the Secretary-General of Komeito), and Nikai (then the Secretary-General of Conservative Party). They continue, "These three politicians, after coming back Japan, couldn't enter in the Diet building because they might have been infected with SARS virus, but they assured the people of Beijing. We Chinese owe a deep obligation to them. And afterwards, Mr. Nikai would always come to aide us when we Chinese suffered. So, media has paid attention to him and reported his activities. Now, Mr. Nikai is the most famous Japanese in China".

In 2015, Nikai (then, the General Affairs Council chief) led 3,000 representative persons of Japanese people to visit Beijing and talked with President Xi Jinping. A Chinese scholar whom I met with shortly afterwards told me as follows.

"In the leadership of China, there was a discussion on whether it would be appropriate President Xi would meet with Mr. Nikai, then the General Affairs Council chief of LDP. And I suppose the deciding factor was the fact that Mr. Nikai was well-known in China. Especially, when the 2008 Sichuan earthquake happened, he visited China with a lot of relief material, and the Chinese people knew it well. I believe this fact was the key factor that President Xi decided to meet with Mr. Nikai. Mr. Nikai is a special figure for the Chinese people".

When I attended at the memorial service for the victims of the Sichuan earthquake held in Chengdu, Sichuan Province, I confirmed in person that the Chinese people respected Nikai extraordinarily.

If the Prime Minister Suga visits China now, he might be able to hold the summit talks with President Xi, but fruitful dialogue may not be so likely. The leaders of China know well the daily words and deeds of leading politicians of Japan. When Abe Shinzo, the former Prime Minister, visited China, he talked with Xi, but it was nothing more than the formality.

However, if Secretary-General Nikai visits China, he can hold fruitful talks with Xi. And it seems unlikely that any Japanese other than the Emperor, Prime Minister Suga, and Nikai can meet and talk with Xi. I believe no Japanese politicians, except Nikai, are able to hold fruitful and specific talks with the Chinese leaders. Secretary-General Nikai is the important key person who connects Japan and China.

In the relationship between Japan and China as well, Nikai is the successor of Tanaka Kakuei.

Chapter 3

Nikai's outstanding political ability with which he exerted his keen intuition to realize the "100,000 yen benefit to every citizen" at the last moment, save people's lives and assure the people

"Only the lives are holy. The love for the living is the prime virtue" ——
Romain Rolland

1. Nikai's covert efforts to overcome the Covid-19 catastrophe

Since January 2020, the main topics of the world have been "Covid-19 catastrophe" and "Trump". And as of May 2021, the Covid-19 catastrophe still continues. After the first and second wave, the third has happened and is more serious than the past waves. Furthermore, it hasn't subsided yet and has been expanding in some area.

Trump, another topic of the world news, lost the presidential election held on November 3rd 2020 and left his position as the President at the end of January 2021. U.S. entered into the era of Biden.

Meanwhile, the new coronavirus infection started in Wuhan, China, and spread worldwide.

It was mid-January 2020 when information about the new coronavirus infection reached Japan. The Ministry of Health, Labour and Welfare announced that a man who had come back from Wuhan turned out positive; thus, the first coronavirus patient was confirmed in Japan.

On January 22nd, Chinese government blocked the city of Wuhan, which had been considered as the source of the new viral pneumonia. On January 25th, the patient of the new viral pneumonia exceeded 1,200 and 41 people had died by then. And on January 29th, the number of the new viral pneumonia patients exceeded that of SARS.

On January 30th, WHO (World Health Organization) declared the state of the emergency.

In Japan, a charter airplane flew to Wuhan on January 29th in order to evacuate the Japanese people there.

In February, panic spread throughout Japan due to the shortage of masks. And it was confirmed that there were ten Covid-19 patients on a cruise ship anchored off the shore of Yokohama port. And on mid-

February, the first fatality from Covid-19 was reported.

At the end of February, the governor of Hokkaido declared the state of the emergency.

During those days, Prime Minister Abe often proceeded with haphazard measures which lacked cool-headedness. The failure of distributing masks, which were mocked as "Abeno-Mask", to every household and the decision of closing all schools without consulting the Ministry of Education, Culture, Sports, Science and Technology were criticized bitterly.

In China, the infection spread further and on February 8th, the victims reached 811 and exceeded the number of the victims from SARS worldwide. WHO named the new coronavirus "Covid-19" and the pandemic spread from China to Europe. In Italy, the number of the infected exccedcd 10,000 on March 10, and it was confirmed that the number was next to that in China.

On March 12th, WHO declared the pandemic.

On March 13th, President Trump declared the state of the national emergency. The infected people increased sharply in U.S. and the number become the largest in the world.

In Japan, on March 5th, the Japanese government announced the postponement of President Xi's official visit to Japan. The National High School Baseball Invitational Tournament of this year was cancelled, and 2020 Summer Olympics and Paralympics in Tokyo were postponed for one year. Then, Tokyo and surrounding four prefectures issued a joint announcement calling for self-curfew.

In April, the number of the infected people worldwide exceeded one million and the fatalities fifty thousand. Furthermore, the fatalities in U.S. exceeded twenty thousand in mid-April and the number of the infected people worldwide exceeded two million.

The Japanese government declared the state of the emergency on April 7th. Then, on April 17th, Prime Minister Abe retracted the "conditional benefit of 300,000 yen", which the cabinet had decided, and officially announced the "100,000 yen benefit to every citizen".

This change of the cabinet decision was realized due to the efforts of Secretary-General Nikai and Yamaguchi Natsuo, the leader of Komeito, and the Abe Cabinet could overcome the crisis of the government thanks to them. The majority of people accepted it and the government could maintain its credibility.

On May 9th, the number of the infected people worldwide exceeded four million, the third of which were reported in U.S. On May 30th, President Trump announced the walkout from WHO, intensifying the tension between U.S. and China further.

At the end of June, the number of the infected people exceeded ten million, and in Japan, the newly infected people were increasing by more than one hundred per day.

At the end of August, Prime Minister Abe announced his resignation due to illness.

In mid-September, Suga Yoshihide, the former chief Cabinet secretary, was appointed as the new Prime Minister.

In early October, it was reported that President Trump had been infected with Covid-19. He was admitted into a hospital but left in just three days and continued his campaign for the election.

In the U.S. presidential election held on November 3rd, Biden defeated Trump.

In mid-November, the Covid-19 infection spread in France, and in Japan as well, the number of the infected people increased sharply at the end of this month. The number worldwide exceeded sixty million.

Thus, the "third wave" emerged.

In 2021, both the world and Japan must dedicate themselves to overcome the Covid-19 catastrophe.

Meanwhile, Nikai has been making efforts behind the scene to support the initiative of the government and local autonomous bodies.

Nikai has been lending a helping hand to Nisaka Yoshinobu, the governor of Wakayama Prefecture who attained some progress in tackling the infection, and delivering necessary material to Wakayama in a discreet way. It is nothing other than Nikai's way of doing something.

During January and February 2020, when the infection had not spread in Japan yet, Nikai cooperated with Tokyo prefecture to send medical material to China to support it. In return, China sent a lot of masks to Nikai when Japan suffered from serious shortage of masks. Nikai provided them for the doctor's organization and local autonomous bodies.

Throughout the year 2020, various trials and errors have been repeated and everyone has made efforts to overcome the Covid-19 catastrophe. Though there were a lot of failures, medical staffs, the government, local governments, and private enterprises have exerted themselves seriously. However, the Covid-19 catastrophe will continue.

Nikai has been supporting the efforts of the government, local autonomous bodies and medical staffs from behind the scene discreetly, and he has been acting up to humanitarianism and preaching the importance of international and domestic cooperation.

In 2021 as well, the biggest challenge for humankind is to overcome the Covid-19 catastrophe, and it is important that everyone cooperates both in the international community and domestically. And Nikai has been working behind the scene for the harmonious cooperation.

2. Nikai's "outstanding political art" by which he overturned even the cabinet decision in order to realize the "100,000 yen benefit to every citizen"

The dominant players for the "100,000 yen benefit to every citizen", which was implemented as one of the important measures against the Covid-19 infection (which had to overturn the official decision made by the cabinet), were Nikai Toshihiro, the Secretary-General of LDP, and Yamaguchi Natsuo, the leader of Komeito. And the factor which led to it was Nikai's statement that the cabinet should change its decision. Yamaguchi took this opportunity, and they realized the grand transformation of the policy.

In a book titled 'I ask Komeito—the direction of this country', which was published on September 20th 2020, Tawara Soichiro and Yamaguchi dialogued, and here I quote the part in which they discussed the activities of Yamaguchi.

Tawara: When you were demanding of Mr. Abe, Mr. Nikai, the Secretary-General of LDP, also referred to the 100,000 yen benefit with an income limit.
Yamaguchi: Yes, that's right.
Tawara: Was Nikai aligning with you?
Yamaguchi: No, we were not. I was surprised a bit because he suddenly held a press conference and referred to the 100,000 yen benefit. However, I changed my mind that we should choose the 100,000 yen benefit instead, because even Mr. Nikai referred to it. I thought that I had to look at the situation calmly and talk with Prime Minister in person, so on the morning of the next day, after we discussed in a conference of Komeito officials, I contacted Mr. Abe and offered suggestions.
Tawara: I see. Then, were you discussing this matter within Komeito?
Yamaguchi: In fact, the plan of the 100,000 yen benefit had already been discussed within our party and we had offered suggestions to the government.
Tawara: Was it earlier than Mr. Nikai referred to it?
Yamaguchi: Yes, it was. By the time Prime Minister Abe announced the plan for the first supplementary budget on March 28th, there was a framework to pay the benefit to each household. But on March 31st, Komeito suggested a plan of the 100,000 yen benefit to every citizen. Then, LDP offered similar suggestions. And a paper reported that Mr. Abe also had had an idea that 100,000 yen should be paid to each person, without any income limit. However, it was overturned by the Ministry of Finance. Saito Tetsuo, the Secretary-General of Komeito, persisted with it, but he could just increase the child benefit by 10,000 yen, reported the

paper. LDP hoped it, Komeito demanded it, and Prime Minister Abe had similar idea. Then, who made a plan to pay the benefit of 300,000 yen to each household? So I demanded of Mr. Abe strongly, saying, "Do you think it is acceptable?"

Tawara: I see. I wonder a little why Mr. Abe accepted what you said. Mr. Yamaguchi, you were hinting at the dissolution of the coalition, weren't you?

Yamaguchi: No way. I didn't say such a thing (laughter). At that time, such stories were reported often, but I never mentioned the dissolution of the coalition. However, I said to Mr. Abe that the confidence in the government would be shaken greatly if he misread public sentiment. Especially after the government declared the state of the emergency, the situation changed significantly. So, I said that if he paid the 300,000 yen benefit only to the households whose income decreased, it would fall into disrepute and few would be happy and feel that they were saved by the government.

Tawara: How long did the talk take between you and Mr. Abe?

Yamaguchi: Well, I think it was about half an hour. What I emphasized was that open communication within the government and the ruling parties wasn't enough and had become difficult. There were some phenomena in which the voice of the people hadn't reached the government adequately. So I asked Mr. Abe to catch the voice of the people enough. If the government altered the policy, from the 300,000 yen benefit to the households whose income decreased to the 100,000 yen benefit to every citizen, it would cause a large scale confusion. Then, Mr. Abe retorted, saying that it would make someone lose face or the passage of the budget would be delayed. Though, I carefully suggested solutions for each of these concerns. For example, I said with confidence and evidence that we would be able to pass the budget if we initiated it now, not after the Golden Week holidays.

Tawara: The change of the policy from the 300,000 yen benefit to the 100,000 yen benefit to every citizen was a major decision for you as well, wasn't it?

Yamaguchi: Of course it was, because I was one of the people who had been responsible for deciding the 300,000 yen benefit. I had to change this policy, so I was ready to swallow my pride to offer the suggestions. Some called it "overturning the table", and it was so indeed. However, it is absolutely better to follow the voice of the people and pay the 100,000 yen benefit than to continue the previous plan irresponsibly knowing we shouldn't do it. I faced with Mr. Abe with a strong belief that the people would definitely value it.

(From 'I ask Komeito—the direction of this country', pp. 92-95)

After deciding to talk with Prime Minister Abe in person, Yamaguchi, the leader of Komeito, met with him on April 15th, and on the next day, telephoned to him and urged strongly.

On this, Yamaguchi said as follows. (ibid. p. 96)

"I carefully explained what Prime Minister was concerned one by one and urged him to decide. Then, in the evening of the same day, the 100,000 yen benefit to every citizen was decided".

It was unusual in the political world that the cabinet decision of the "300,000 yen benefit to the households whose income had been decreased" was changed to the "100,000 yen benefit to every citizen", but as a result, the Abe administration was able to get out of trouble due to this shift of policy. If they had forced the "300,000 yen benefit", the distrust of the people against Abe administration must have grown and the administration would have been put in an extremely difficult position. Thus it can be said Yamaguchi saved the Abe administration.

I once heard from a staff of Komeito that young and middle-ranking Diet members of Komeito had strongly criticized the "300,000 benefit to the households whose income had been decreased". The main critic was Okamoto Mitsunari (Lower House member) and it was he who led the shift to the "100,000 benefit to every citizen".

On April 14th, Nikai said in a press conference, "There are sincere requests for the 100,000 yen benefit to every citizen. So I will strongly ask the government to implement what they can as soon as possible". And this statement led to the change of the cabinet decision.

Shortly after that, Komeito stepped into action and launched an intensive offensive. In the morning of April 15th, Yamaguchi, in an interview with Prime Minister Abe which was held on a short notice, strongly asked him to "pay the 100,000 yen benefit to every citizen without any income limit". And what happened afterwards was as mentioned above.

Nikai, the Secretary-General of LDP, and Yamaguchi, the leader of Komeito, stepped separate paths but, by launching an offensive at the same moment, accomplished the change of the cabinet decision. Some called it "A and Un breathing (perfect timing in a collaboration)" and it might be right.

3. The switch from "conditional 300,000 yen benefit" to "100,000 yen to every citizen"

On April 3rd, the government determined the framework for the payment of cash to the households whose income had been decreased due to the spread of Covid-19 infection. Its contents were, "The benefit will be 300,000 yen per household. The subject will be the households whose monthly income falls below a certain level and the benefit will not be paid to high-income earners. Those who receive the benefit shall apply in the office of their city, town, or village".

On the same day, Prime Minister Abe talked with Kishida Fumio, the Policy Affairs Research Council chief of LDP, in the office of Prime Minister and told him his intention that the benefit would be 300,000 yen per household. After this meeting, Kishida told the reporters that his intention was the same with that of Prime Minister and Abe agreed with it.

Media reported that it was decided by the leadership of Prime Minister Abe, Vice Prime Minister and Finance Minister Aso, and Policy

Affairs Research Council chief Kishida. On April 7th, the Abe Cabinet determined the supplementary budget bill which included the "conditional benefit of 300,000 yen", but at this moment, complaints erupted among the people.

The plan for the "100,000 yen benefit to every citizen" had already been widely known. Not only opposition parties but Komeito insisted on the 100,000 yen benefit to every citizen. The "conditional benefit of 300,000 yen" upset the people and they showed strong disgruntlement against the Abe administration. Both LDP and Komeito could not ignore such strong objections by the people.

The words which Nikai told reporters on April 14th were very finely timed; they made Komeito step into motion quickly, then Yamaguchi talked with Prime Minister Abe in person and the switch of the cabinet decision was accomplished.

"Politics is not science but art" was a phrase by Bismarck, a great statesman of 19th century Germany. A skillful politician equips him with the "art".

Miki Bukichi, the key player of the merger of conservative parties in 1955, was a master of this "art" as well and Tanaka Kakuei also used it skillfully. Furthermore, Nikai is the most skillful master of this "art" in the present and adept at using it.

To the "art" which Nikai used, Yamaguchi responded with the "A and Un breathing", and it saved Abe administration from the crisis. The distrust of the people against the government calmed down and the sense of "relief" spread. And the people accepted the decision of "100,000 yen benefit to every citizen".

An aide of Nikai said to me, "Mr. Nikai always looks at the whole people carefully and studies the trend of the world. He considers not only the present but also the future. He has a broad view and looks at not only near places but also distant places. Mr. Nikai is a great politician capable of deciding with a bird's-eye view".

Nikai masters the "art of politics" and at the same time has a genius faculty of "inspiration" and an ability to read someone's minds. This ability was exerted when the "100,000 yen benefit to every citizen" was decided.

Nikai has exerted his leadership for the policies and issues of the Suga administration as well. Right after its formation, the Suga Cabinet has focused on relatively minute issues in order to achieve something specific as soon as possible, whereas Secretary-General Nikai has tackled bigger themes and supported the Suga administration.

What Nikai is tackling now is an economic policy for the future; he has suggested large scale additional economic measures in order to avert a great recession. Furthermore, he believes that Japan should act as an intermediary for the reconciliation between U.S. and China. The Secretary-General of LDP himself plans to visit these two countries and act as an intermediary for them. In addition, he considers improving Japan's relationship with China and South Korea as well as visiting North Korea. Thus, the excellent leadership of Nikai will be exerted in the terms of international relations as well.

Chapter 4

The true image of Secretary-General Nikai described by his closest aides—The origin of his genius political "intuition", his way of human diplomacy, deep love for his home Wakayama and great contribution to it, and "Nikai-ism" in which he has always dedicated himself for others

"To do easily what is difficult for others is the mark of talent. To do what is impossible for talent is the mark of genius" ——*Amiel*

1. The true image of Nikai described by Hayashi Motoo, the Acting Secretary-General and the best and brightest comrade of Nikai

(1) Hayashi Motoo is the best and brightest comrade of Nikai

An excellent leader invariably has an excellent aide, and whether a top leader can achieve something or not depends on whether he is blessed with an excellent aide.

In the past, powerful politicians invariably had excellent aides. For example, there were Miki Bukichi and Kono Ichiro under Hatoyama Ichiro, Ikeda Hayato and Sato Eisaku under Yoshida Shigeru, Maeo Shigesaburo, Ohira Masayoshi, and Miyazawa Kiichi under Ikeda Hayato, and Hashimoto Tomisaburo, Nikaido Susumu, Esaki Masumi, and Takashita Noboru under Tanaka Kakuei.

Looking back the 75 years after the World War II, the best combination of a leader and an aide before Nikai Toshihiro and Hayashi Motoo was Ishibashi Tanzan and Ishida Hirohide. However, this combination was short-lived because Ishibashi retired from office due to illness.

The combination of Nikai and Hayashi is as good and excellent as that of Ishibashi and Ishida.

During these ten years, I have often met with Nikai and Hayashi in person, and it seems that Nikai and Hayashi share the one and same character. I have sometimes felt that they are in fact one person named "Nikaibayashi Toshimoto (Nikaibayashi = Nikai + Hayashi, Toshimoto = Toshihiro + Motoo)". They are allies, comrades, a teacher and a pupil, brothers, and more than those.

Nikai is a great statesman. In an Aristotle way, he is one of the most excellent politicians with the prerogative of logic and intelligence who are always serving people. And Hayashi totally fell in love with Nikai and has dedicated himself to realize the politics of Nikai as his aide.

What distinguishes Hayashi is the fact that he has never left Nikai alone. Hayashi is always with Nikai and supports him carefully. Nikai also trusts Hayashi completely. Such a trustful relationship as that of Nikai and Hayashi might be quite rare in the history of politics. Hayashi is a politician who knows Nikai inside out. I am aware of Hayashi's way of life, "consistent sincerity and loyalty", and deeply respect him.

Here I quote the testimony of Hayashi which he told me.

(2) An outstanding master of political "intuition" and "inspiration"

What Secretary-General Nikai excels in is his political "intuition" and inspiration. They are not something which can be learned from someone, and I believe he was born equipped with them.

There are three examples in which Mr. Nikai exerted his political "intuition".

First, shortly after he became the Secretary-General, Mr. Nikai extended the term of LDP president. In those days, the majority of LDP members considered that they should not replace the president at the end of his second term, that is, in six years.

Thus, Mr. Nikai set up a study committee with the then vice president Kohmura as its chairman and asked the members to hold the committee once a week and consider various possibilities.

What Nikai thought was as follows. "The LDP president is also the Prime Minister, so he would face a lot of difficulties and, if the party lose a Lower House election, he has to accept the blame. And there is an Upper House election as well. If he fails in the management of Diet, he has to choose between the dissolution of Lower House and the en masse resignation of the cabinet. If he loses an election, he cannot maintain the position of Prime Minister and LDP president. If a Prime Minister can overcome such difficulties, we should extend the term of the president and let him maintain this position repeatedly".

After two months of intensive discussions, we decided to extend the term of the president to three terms nine years.

I was totally amazed and thought that this political "intuition", perfect timing, and speediness is the essence of Nikai Toshihiro. Thanks to this amendment, Mr. Abe could break the record of the longest tenure by Katsura Taro and Sato Eisaku.

Second is the "100,000 yen benefit" in 2020, one of the measures against Covid-19. The government and the ruling parties had decided the "300,000 yen benefit with limitation" in the cabinet. When we initiated this plan, Mr. Nikai suddenly said in a press conference that 100,000 yen might be better. This one word from the Secretary-General of LDP spread across the political community quickly and the atmosphere changed totally. As a result, the government cancelled its original plan of "300,000 yen" and adopted the "100,000 yen benefit" instead. It is unprecedented that a cabinet decision was overturned.

After the government decided the 300,000 yen benefit, a lot of voices from the people reached the party. However, Secretary-General Nikai discussed with no one, even with the Prime Minister, the Minister of Finance, or anyone in the party, and mentioned it in the press conference. This is truly the political "intuition" of Secretary-General Nikai. And timing was perfect as well.

On the next morning, Mr. Yamaguchi, the leader of Komeito, visited the office of Prime Minister and strongly demanded Prime Minister Abe to adopt the "100,000 yen benefit". In this way, the "100,000 yen benefit" was realized.

Afterwards, Prime Minister Abe said, "if it were not for Secretary-General Nikai's words in the press conference, we would have been faced with extreme difficulties. I would like to thank him because the face of the government and LDP was maintained".

In this case, too, Mr. Nikai wasn't asked by someone to do so but exerted his own "intuition."

Just before that press conference, I, the Acting Secretary-General, asked Mr. Nikai to talk about Avigan in it. Although he did so, this topic was overlooked because the reporters focused on the issue of "100,000 yen".

Third is the LDP presidential election on September 2020 which selected the successor of Prime Minister Abe. On August 28th, he told Mr. Nikai that he would resign due to illness. For it was a matter of health, we couldn't ask him to remain in this position. So we held the officers' meeting quickly and Mr. Nikai assumed the role of managing the presidential election.

In the evening of the next day, August 29th, Suga Yoshihide, then the chief Cabinet secretary, told me that he would like to meet with Secretary-General Nikai. So they met secretly and Mr. Suga said that he would run for the presidential election and politely asked Mr. Nikai for his support. Then Mr. Nikai answered instantly, "Okay. Go get 'em, and I will support you.", and decided to support Mr. Suga as Nikai faction. Mr. Nikai is speedy when doing something.

This time, too, Nikai didn't discussed with anyone, but the members of Nikai faction quickly agreed on supporting Mr. Suga. In just two days of the weekend, it created the trend of supporting Mr. Suga. I think other factions and groups were planning to move from Monday. Thus, the trend for "LDP president Suga" was made by Nikai's feat of agility. It was also the political "intuition" of Mr. Nikai, and the timing was perfect, too.

Mr. Nikai has exerted his political "intuition" in the relationship with China as well. It was in 2015 when he was the General Affairs Council chief of LDP.

At that time, the relationship between Japan and China was still strained. Even when Prime Minister Abe and President Xi Jinping held talks, their relationship was so strained that they shook hands avoiding eye contact. Then, as the General Affairs Council chief, Mr. Nikai led a delegation consisted of 3,000 people to Beijing. And in front of the 3,000 people, Mr. Nikai and President Xi shook hands and made speech. It was the beginning of improving the relationship between Japan and China.

Next year, when the "World Forum of Belt and Road Initiative" was about to be held in Beijing, both U.S. and Japanese governments announced that they would not participate in it. However, China sent the invitation letter to Mr. Nikai. By then, Nikai had already become the Secretary-General, and he answered that he would visit Beijing and attend the forum. Hearing this, the cabinet members were annoyed and hinted that they hoped Mr. Nikai wouldn't attend, though Mr. Nikai himself believed that he must participate in it.

Then, Sakakibara Sadayuki, then the chairperson of Japan Business Federation, told that he would like to join the "Nikai mission". This changed the situation totally; Matsumura Yoshifumi, the State Minister of Economy, Trade and Industry, and finally, Imai Takaya, a secretary of the Prime Minister, asked Mr. Nikai to include them in the mission. Mr. Nikai is generous, so he said that all those who wanted to join the mission could do so.

At the meeting with President Xi, Mr. Nikai expressed his idea, saying, "Japan and China are neighbors and cannot move away. So we have to be intimate. And to be intimate, the mutual traffic is essential. I would like to focus my efforts on the exchange of the youth. How do you think?" President Xi answered, "I agree with you. Let's proceed with it".

Mr. Nikai's belief is that the trust and human relations between not only the leaders but also the people of both countries are important, and by deepening them, we can strengthen the peaceful and friendly relationship.

Usually, if the office of Prime Minister asks a party officer not to go, he will not go. However, Mr. Nikai was different and acted with the belief that he had to visit China right now. It is the political "intuition" of Mr. Nikai.

Mr. Nikai always says, "Just saying something is not enough. Do it," and does so himself. He always makes decisions instantly and it is his way.

Mr. Nikai is an excellent idea person. For example, when someone talks about the recreation of the rural areas, he would say, "Let's hold a product exhibition then" and such exhibitions would be held soon in the entrance hall of LDP headquarters to advertise unique products of the prefecture. Now, every prefecture competes to hold it.

The first prefecture which held an exhibition was Wakayama, the home of Mr. Nikai, and the sales were good. Then, the Prime Minister Abe suggested Yamaguchi Prefecture hold an exhibition as well. Because the Prime Minister sold products himself, everyone bought them. The sales of Yamaguchi Prefecture surpassed that of Wakayama and rose to the top.

Hokkaido held an exhibition as well. For it is blessed with excellent seafood and mountain food, its sales surpassed that of Yamaguchi and rose to the top.

As for the matter of agriculture, young Diet members of LDP know neither actual agriculture, rice planting, nor harvesting. That's not good. Thus, we concluded that they should experience agriculture and started it in three Tama areas and Saitama Prefecture in collaboration with agricultural cooperative societies there. I said planting by hand was fundamental and took the initiative. We did harvesting using sickles. When we hold agriculture experience in Tokyo, we approach Diet members of Tokyo, and when we hold it in Saitama, we approach Diet members of Saitama. Then, thirty to forty people would participate in it. We have held harvest festivals and rice cake making festivals as well.

While Mr. Nikai is an idea person, he does anything quickly. This is his way.

(3) Nikai formulated three lawmaker-initiated bills when LDP was an opposition party

Mr. Nikai formulated three lawmaker-initiated bills when LDP was an opposition party: "the Act on Promotion of Tsunami Countermeasures", "the Act on Special Measures for Prevention of Damage Related to Agriculture, Forestry and Fisheries Caused by Wildlife", and "the Act on Prevention of illegal private download." In addition, he formulated the Act for National Resilience Contributing to Preventing and Mitigating Disasters, the Act on Countermeasures Against Tokyo Inland Earthquake

and the Act on Countermeasures Against Nankai Trough Earthquake, but
LDP regained power on the way, so they were enacted after LDP became
the ruling party.

I am proud that Mr. Nikai and I could have three lawmaker-initiated
bills enacted when LDP was an opposition party. When I said to Mr. Nikai
that submitting the bill would be enough, he scolded me, saying, "Do not
be stupid. Anyone can submit a bill, but if you submit a bill, you must
enact it". I answered, "Mr. Nikai, now we hold only 119 seats in the Lower
House, while DPJ holds more than 300. It is impossible". However, Mr.
Nikai said, "It is not impossible. What is necessary is necessary. Everyone
will understand it. Do it". Thus, we stepped into action, but anyone would
just ignore an opposition party with only 119 seats. The regular Diet
session ended, and our efforts didn't bear fruit in the next extraordinary
session. At first, we were ignored by everybody, but we didn't give up and
visited various DPJ Diet members.

Then, "Great East Japan earthquake" occurred and many were
killed by the tsunami. I lost heart and regretted that if we had taken
more measures via the Act, the number of the victims could have been
decreased. I suggested to Mr. Nikai to give up the enactment of the Act,
but he answered, "Don't be silly. A tight spot is also an opportunity. Let's
go ahead now" and continued to visit the Diet members of DPJ.

Later, DPJ presented their own plan. The contents were the same with
those of ours, but in their plan, the "Day of Tsunami" was March 11th. In
our plan, it was November 5th, the date of the "Fire of Shock". So, by the
suggestion from Mr. Nikai, we collected the opinions of learned persons,
and most of them supported "November 5th"; they said that "March
11th" was the day of eulogy, so they weren't sure whether the date was
appropriate for the "Day of Tsunami". Meanwhile, November 5th is the
day of a successful experience, the "Fire of Shock". Mr. Nikai persuaded
the Diet members of DPJ, and finally it agreed to make November 5th the
"Day of Tsunami". However, DPJ demanded that it be the proposition by
the committee chairperson, not by LDP. When I reported it to Mr. Nikai,

he said, "Okay, let's take the profit over the fame. The proposition by the committee chairperson is just fine. However, all the parties should take part in the discussion. The process of the enactment of the Act on Measures against Tsunami must be recorded. If we have the record, we can pass it down to later generations". Mr. Nikai can make such decision quickly; it is a genuine politician.

Mr. Nikai continued, "Let's have the Diet members of our faction visit the embassies in Tokyo and ask for the establishment of the 'World Tsunami Awareness Day'". And after the regular session, he told the Diet members who had won elections less than four times to visit the embassies in Tokyo. Each MP visited five or six embassies with a brochure written in English and asked the diplomats to convey the proposition to their home countries. The Ministry of Foreign Affairs turned pale, because they had to prepare translators of not only English but also other languages; the Ministry got to take it seriously.

They were surprised to see the brochure written in English because there was a sentence which asked other countries to join the co-sponsors. Mr. Nikai asked them not only to support the proposition but to join the co-sponsors of it.

As a result, the "World Tsunami Awareness Day: November 5th" was passed unanimously in the U.N. General Assembly held in the end of December.

Yet it did not stop there. Mr. Nikai proposed the "World Summit by high school students" to celebrate the establishment of the "World Tsunami Awareness Day". It was proceeded quickly as well; the summit, in which all participants spoke English, was successful, with high school students from twenty-five countries present, and has continued to this day.

Mr. Nikai said, "those high school students from all over the world are civil ambassadors." If high school students from the world come to Japan, learn about Japan, and feet that Japan is a wonderful country, they will all be civil ambassadors who see Japan favorably. He explained to President Xi the importance of exchanges by the youth and has increased future civil ambassadors.

Mr. Nikai always says that politics is practice and acts so himself. I can learn a lot of things from him, such as that speeches are not enough in politics but practice is important. I can feel the excellence of Mr. Nikai.

(4) Nikai has been active in the front line as an expert of disaster-prevention

"Great East Japan earthquake" occurred when LDP was an opposition party. Then, an official of Japan Business Federation asked Nikai a favor, saying, "we want to deliver oil and gasoline to the affected areas. However, since they are hazardous material, the police permission is necessary, but there are some obstacles for it. Could you lend a hand for us?"

Then, Mr. Nikai told me, "you had once served as the National Public Safety Commissioner, so please negotiate with the police". I happened to be acquainted with the Deputy Vice-Minister, so I talked to him about it. Though he answered that it might take some time, but the permission was granted soon, and tank trucks conveying petrol and gasoline were able to run on the expressways as early as in the evening of the day. I felt that the police moved rather quickly for them, despite the fact that we were an opposition party at that time.

There are many cases in which I have felt the excellence of Mr. Nikai. For example, when "Great East Japan earthquake" occurred, he was concerned about coffin. He said that a lot of coffins would be needed in such a large-scale earthquake and ordered twenty thousand coffins.

The agency which manages coffin is the Ministry of Economy, Trade and Industry and Mr. Nikai knew it. Thus, he demanded the manager in charge to order coffins as soon as possible. Though we were told that only ten thousand coffins were available, we ordered twenty thousand of them, saying makeshift ones were okay. However, the coffins were still not enough.

When LDP was an opposition party, I acted along with Mr. Nikai almost every day. We worked for the measures against disasters, passed the three lawmaker-initiated bills, and received many requests from various groups of the people. Though members of an opposition party, we were very busy.

We, members of LDP, were frequently asked to deliver relief supplies to the self defense force. DPJ, the ruling party then, was inexperienced, so they relied on LDP even when it was an opposition party. We received various request and made arrangements for them.

When it comes to disaster, it is Mr. Nikai whom one can trust the most; everyone knows that he is the most prominent politician in the area of disaster. When "Great Hanshin-Awaji earthquake" happened, Mr. Nikai, though a member of an opposition party, arrived at the affected area faster than anyone else, delivered relief supplies, and did rescue activities. Furthermore, he has published a book about disaster. Mr. Nikai is really quick in doing something; he steps into action instantly.

Some years ago, when our faction (Shisui-kai = Nikai faction) held a workshop in Hokkaido, we are hit by a typhoon on the last day of it. Then, various people including the governor made requests to Mr. Nikai. So we stopped the workshop and went to the affected area together. We received requests from various persons and groups, dealt with them quickly, and went to the affected sites. Mr. Nikai is a man who acts instantly. It is his habit, and he is by no means an ordinary politician.

(5) Nikai's diplomacy is always human diplomacy

Mr. Nikai does his political activities placing human relations at their center. He creates trust relationship and does activities based on it. It applies to elections, political activities in Tokyo, and diplomatic activities as well.

Mr. Nikai is engaged in diplomatic activities based on the trust relationship. When he visited China, South Korea, Vietnam, Indonesia and so on, he did diplomatic activities using mainly human relationship.

Mr. Nikai has talked with President Xi five times. No one else has met with him so frequently except the former Prime Minister Abe. Whereas

Mr. Abe talked with President Xi officially, Mr. Nikai met with him through the personal trust relationship. Japanese politicians who have met with President Xi more than once are only Mr. Abe and Mr. Nikai, but Mr. Nikai never boasts about it; he has always been engaged in his diplomatic activities based on human relationship.

When Mr. Nikai met with Prime Minister Phúc of Vietnam, human relationship was at the center of it. It began with the "lotus diplomacy". Mr. Nikai had presented Oga lotus and Mr. Phúc sent Vietnamese lotus in return; it was an exchange of lotus. The Vietnamese lotus was planted in Kinokawa, Wakayama Prefecture, and has bloomed there. Mr. Nikai invited Prime Minister Phúc to Kinokawa to show the lotus flower from Vietnam. It was when Osaka Summit was held.

Then, Prime Minister Phúc invited Mr. Nikai to Vietnam, so he visited his home on January 2020 with the delegation consisting of 1,000 people. In this way, the relationship between Mr. Nikai and Prime Minister Phúc has been deepened further.

The political activities of Mr. Nikai, both international and domestic, are based on human relationship and trust relationship. This manner of action never changes; he is always sincere.

Mr. Nikai has many friends in China, South Korea, Vietnam, Indonesia, and other countries, supporting and interacting with them with trust relationship. His diplomacy is humanistic at all times, and I always learn from him how a politician should be. Mr. Nikai is really a great statesman.

2. The testimony of Koizumi Ryuji, the chief of International Bureau of LDP—Nikai Diplomacy is human diplomacy based on trust relationship

(1) Koizumi Ryuji, the chief of International Bureau who is responsible for the diplomatic activities of LDP

Koizumi Ryuji, the chief of International Bureau of LDP, is one of the closest aides of Nikai and his loyal adviser, as well as a superb politician with incomparable sincerity.

One of the most important characteristics of Nikai's politics is that it has diplomatic capability; "Nikai Diplomacy" has played a large part in the Japanese politics. Essentially, diplomatic activities that Secretary-General Nikai has been engaged in are to support the diplomacy of the government, but sometimes an aide plays a larger part than the main character, and it applies to the current relationship of Japan with China and South Korea. Nikai's exchanges with China and South Korea have contributed to stopping breakdown of Japan's relationship with these two countries.

It is Koizumi who, along with Kawamura Takeo, the acting chairperson of Shisui-kai, Hayashi Motoo, the acting Secretary-General of LDP, and Yamaguchi Tsuyoshi, the chief vice Secretary-General of LDP (as well as the secretary-general of Shisui-kai), who has been supporting the Nikai Diplomacy.

I became acquainted with Koizumi fifteen years ago, when Koizumi Jyunichiro, the then Prime Minister, dissolved the Lower House for the postal service privatization. Because he opposed to it in spite of being a Lower House member of LDP, Prime Minister Koizumi discarded him and sent a "hit-man". He lost the election by a narrow margin, suffering a setback. However, Koizumi overcame it with his never-dying spirit; later, he consolidated his constituency and has won the elections as an unaffiliated candidate. Then, supported by the LDP branch in his constituency, he returned to the party and has worked under Nikai. Now, he leads LDP's diplomatic activities as an indisputable aide of Nikai.

Koizumi is one of the first-rate politicians in his ethic, in his intelligence, and in that he loves the people; he is a statesman with incomparable sincerity. Koizumi is adept at election campaign as well, so he is expected to become a minister in the next cabinet shuffle.

(2) Koizumi speaks about "Nikai's human diplomacy"

Four years have passed since Mr. Nikai became the Secretary-General of LDP, and diplomatic activities of LDP have become to play a much larger part in the national politics. It can be called a drastic change.

On September 2020, the LDP presidential election was held. Since the president of LDP becomes the Prime Minister, it was in fact an election which would elect the Prime Minister. Then, as a condition of being elected, whether the candidates had "diplomatic experiences" was discussed.

In the past, all politicians were oriented toward domestic politics and those who were adept at it became the top leader. And this trend of emphasizing domestic affairs has continued up to now. However, during the four years since Mr. Nikai became the Secretary-General, the tide of world politics has changed.

The world situation, especially the relationship between U.S. and China, has changed greatly. And the attitude of Japan, which is wedged between these two superpowers, has become to attract more attention from these two countries, as well as Asian and European countries; they are concerned with which direction Japan will proceed to.

In such a situation, the former Prime Minister Abe developed a diplomacy that took a panoramic perspective of the world map. And in it, Secretary-General Nikai was engaged in his own diplomacy, especially with Asian countries such as China and South Korea.

During this period, the awareness of the people has changed as well, and more and more people have learned that diplomacy and domestic politics are the two sides of the same coin. Especially, Mr. Nikai's diplomacy toward China has attracted more attention, and LDP's diplomacy has become to play a larger part.

In the situation where the cold war and unilateral domination by U.S. ended and China gained power, Secretary-General Nikai has developed LDP's diplomacy from the viewpoint of how Japan would protect its national interest. The former Prime Minister Abe as well as the Japanese people accepted his diplomacy, and both the people and politicians has become more concerned with the movement of the world.

Then, on September 2020, the Suga Cabinet was formed by the leadership of Secretary-General Nikai. The U.S. presidential election was held as well, and China has also moved drastically; the world has entered an era of great global transition.

In my opinion, the presence of Secretary-General Nikai has become more important to not only Japanese people but also the U.S. and Chinese governments; it attracts an attention from all over the world.

Also, the world has paid attention to what kind of diplomatic activities Secretary-General Nikai will launch among the trilateralism of Japan, U.S. and China, as well as in South Korea and Asian countries, and how he will move while supporting the diplomacy of the Japanese government.

In 2015, Mr. Nikai, who had not become the Secretary-General yet and acted as the General Affairs Council chief then, visited China with three thousand people and met with President Xi. It was a big event and surprised both China and Japan. Before that, diplomacy had been considered as a task of experts, but Mr. Nikai did civil diplomacy. This Nikai Diplomacy attracted an attention both internationally and domestically and cooled down the tension between Japan and China caused by the issue around Senkaku Islands. It was a historical feat.

Mr. Nikai sometimes says, "if you don't have an influence over domestic politics, you cannot exert an influence over diplomatic affairs as well". It is true, and Nikai Diplomacy proved that if one cannot exert influence in diplomacy, he cannot do so in domestic politics as well".

The relationship between U.S. and China is important in looking at the future world situation. I think the relationship between these two superpowers will not change fundamentally even if the U.S. Presidents change; the anti-China attitude of U.S. will continue.

Considering the Japan-U.S. relationship, Japan-China relationship, and Japan-South Korea relationship, the presence of Secretary-General Nikai has become really big. So it would not be exaggerating to say that he has become to influence on the world situation significantly.

In my view, it is a "mission" given to Mr. Nikai by the heaven that he has been engaged in "diplomacy" as the Secretary-General while supporting the Suga administration.

People seems to think that the diplomacy of Secretary-General Nikai is limited to Asian countries such as China and South Korea, but he has visited U.S. frequently. Thus, he will visit U.S. again when the political situation there calms down. Nikai Diplomacy will spread all over the world.

Recently, Mr. Nikai has often said, "I will visit America first" and "Visit to U.S. precedes visit to China". He thinks seriously how Japan should survive in the conflict between U.S. and China, and I think he will visit U.S. and discuss with the high officials. Then he will establish a relationship between the ruling parties of both countries.

(3) Nikai's unchanging attitude toward diplomacy

Secretary-General Nikai's attitude toward diplomacy never changes. For example, the relationship between Japan and South Korea changes all the time, but Mr. Nikai's attitude is constant. He always says, "China and South Korea are our neighbors. Since a country cannot move away, we have to be friendly with them. The world sees whether Japan can get along with neighboring countries or not. The international trust in Japan depends on it. We have to prove that Japan is a country capable of getting along with neighboring countries".

Now, the relationship between Japan and South Korea has gotten worse, but in the past, when Park Geun-hye was the President, we were getting along with South Korea. However, the attitude of Secretary-

General Nikai hasn't changed a bit. In my view, it is because Mr. Nikai sees anyone as a human that his attitude never changes whether in good times or bad times. What he is engaged in is the "human diplomacy".

Mr. Nikai's attitude never changes whether those politicians he has become acquainted with and befriended success or fail, or even if they are in an unfortunate situation; he never forgets friendship.

Mr. Nikai's attitude toward Mr. Park Jie-won, who was the chief presidential secretary to President Kim Dae-jung and now acts as the Director of the National Intelligence Service under President Moon Jae-in, hasn't changed a bit as well, whatever position Mr. Park is in. When Mr. Park was incarcerated, Mr. Nikai sent three pieces of underwear made from camel's hair. And when Mr. Park was released, Mr. Nikai invited him to Wakayama and entertained him. Furthermore, when Mr. Park fell from power and was isolated in the Diet, the then Vice Minister of Land, Infrastructure and Transport visited him on behalf of Mr. Nikai.

Once Mr. Nikai befriends someone, whether this person is under the scrutiny of the government or in jail means nothing to him. Friendship comes first.

Now, the relationship between Japan and South Korea is on the verge of breakup. However, it hasn't actually broken up yet mainly due to the efforts of Mr. Nikai.

In the relationship with China as well, the presence of Mr. Nikai is really big. When he visits China, he is able to meet with the top officials. Chinese leadership sees Mr. Nikai as someone whom they can truly trust.

The diplomacy of peace and friendship is built on the mutual trust relationship. Both parties have to have respect for the other, but in reality, not a few politicians cannot have such respect. But Mr. Nikai never betrays anyone; he is always sincere.

Recently, some politicians claim loudly that China should not be tolerated, but Mr. Nikai often says to us, "If you think China should not be tolerated, you have to tell the Chinese government so directly. However, no one dares to visit China and tell the Chinese government so. If you make a fuss in Japan only, nothing can't be solved. If it were me, I would visit China and tell directly, and I have been doing so". I believe Mr. Nikai is right.

(4) The unique style of Nikai's diplomacy

The method of Mr. Nikai's diplomacy is unique in that he focuses on the home and origin of the other side.

For example, when Mr. Nikai visited U.S. to meet President Obama, he went to Chicago, the origin of Obama family, first and visited Mr. Obama's office there, then proceeded to Washington.

Similarly, when Mr. Nikai visited China to meet President Xi, he went to Fujian, the home province of Xi family, then proceeded to Beijing. And when he actually met with President Xi, he said, "I went to Fujian. It has been developing significantly, hasn't it?" In this way, he could have a lively conversation naturally.

When Mr. Nikai visited South Korea to meet with President Moon Jae-in, he went to the hometown of the former President Kim Dae-jung, the mentor of Mr. Moon. Then he proceeded to Seoul and met with Mr. Moon.

Any leader in any country has his home and origin and loves his hometown. When Mr. Nikai visits a foreign country, he goes to the home of the leader and pay respect to his hometown or the places which he has some connections with, and then proceed to the talks. By learning about the hometowns of each other, friendship develops.

The human diplomacy of Mr. Nikai attracts attention from the world. And LDP will energetically proceed with diplomatic activities which supplements the governmental diplomacy.

(5) The office of the Secretary-General of LDP is the biggest diplomatic stage in Japan

What is outstanding among Nikai's activities is the diplomatic one as Liberal Democratic Party. Though their purpose is to support and supplement the governmental diplomacy, they attract more attention from the world because they have characteristics of people's diplomacy.

Before Nikai became the Secretary-General, LDP wasn't engaged in diplomatic activities on the basis that the government should be responsible for diplomacy. After Nikai was appointed as the Secretary-General, however, the office of the Secretary-General of LDP has become a stage for diplomatic activities.

The list below shows the history of LDP's diplomacy since 2014, when Nikai acted as the General Affairs Council chief. It also reflects a fact that the perception "The most powerful figure in the political community of Japan is Secretary-General Nikai" has spread throughout the world. Remarkably, high officials of foreign countries who visited Japan went to the office of the Secretary-General of LDP to meet with Nikai. Thus, this list clearly shows that one of the main purposes of those high officials visiting Japan is to meet with Secretary-General Nikai. This fact has never been reported in media, and the list was created by Koizumi Ryuji, the chief of International Bureau of LDP, especially for this book.

When Covid-19 catastrophe calms down and international exchanges resume in the future, more and more foreign leaders will visit the office of the Secretary-General of LDP.

The diplomatic activities by Nikai are "people's diplomacy"; when he visits a foreign country, representatives of various groups, such as economic community, community of local politicians, academic and cultural circle, tourism industry, sports community, gather together and form a large-scale delegation. Secretary-General Nikai always acts with the expansion of people's exchanges in mind. And this fact is the reason that he has gained high and strong trust in foreign countries. Nikai is the promoter of people's diplomacy as well as the great and outstanding leader of it.

The record of Nikai's meeting with important foreign persons

2014 (as the General Affairs Council chief)			
October 20th	Singapore	The ambassador to Japan	Chin Siat Yoon
November 17th	China	The delegate to Japan of International Liaison Department of the Chinese Communist Party	(Headed by Zhao Shitong)
2016 (as the General Affairs Council chief or the Secretary-General)			
April 7th	China	Special Representative of the Chinese Government on the Korean Peninsula Affairs	Wu Dawei
August 10th	China	The ambassador to Japan	Cheng Yonghua
August 29th	Turkey	The ambassador to Japan	Ahmet Bülent Meriç
August 31th	United States	Deputy Chief of Mission for the United States Embassy in Tokyo	Jason Hyland
September 27th	China	The chairperson of China-Japan Friendship Association	Tang Jiaxuan
September 28th	Singapore	Prime Minister	Lee Hsien Loong
October 21st	India	The ambassador to Japan	Sujan Romeshchandra Chinoy
November 10th	Kenya	Speaker of the National Assembly	Justin Muturi
2017 (as the Secretary-General)			
May 15th	South Korea	the presidential envoy	Moon Hee-sang
May 24th	Kazakhstan	First Deputy Chairman, Nur-Otan Party	Mukhtar Kul-Mukhammed
May 30th	China	State councillor	Yang Jiechi
July 13th	Indonesia	Minister for public projects and national housing	Basuki Hadimoeljono
August 28th	Indonesia	Secretary-General of Indonesian Democratic Party of Struggle	Hasto Kristiyanto
September 8th	United States	The ambassador to Japan	William Francis Hagerty
September 19th	South Korea	The ambassador to Japan	Lee Joon-gyu
September 22th	Turkey	The ambassador to Japan	Ahmet Bülent Meriç
November 22th	Nepal	The ambassador to Japan	Prativa Rana
November 24th	South Korea	The ambassador to Japan	Lee Su-hoon
November 28th	Indonesia	Minister of Trade	Enggartiasto Lukita

December 8th	China	Chairperson of China Center for International Economic Exchanges	Zeng Peiyan
December 15th	Venezuela	The ambassador to Japan	Seiko Luis Ishikawa Kobayashi
2018 (as the Secretary-General)			
January 22nd	China	the vice-chairman of the Standing Committee of the National People's Congress	Chen Zhu
March 1st	Turkey	The ambassador to Japan	Hasan Murat Mercan
March 13th	Russia	The ambassador to Japan	Mikhail Galuzin
March 13th	Turkey	Minister of Economy	Nihat Zeybekci
April 4th	Turkey	Deputy Prime Minister	Recep Akdag
April 16th	South Korea	The chairperson of Korea-Japan Parliamentarians' Union	Kang Chang-il
April 17th	China	State Councilor	Wang Yi
April 18th	China	former State Councilor	Dai Bingguo
May 8th	China	The delegation led by the Governor of Sichuan	Yin Li
May 9th	China	Governor of Liaoning	Tang Yijun
		The delegation led by the mayor of Dalian	Tan Chengxu
May 10th	China	Premier of the State Council	Li Keqiang
May 11th	China	Minister of Culture and Tourism	Luo Shugang
June 21st	China	The chairperson of China Association for International Friendly Contact	Chen Yuan
July 2nd	Burnei	Minister of Foreign Affairs II	Erywan Pehin Yusof
August 22nd	China	Counselor and Chief of Mission for the China Embassy in Tokyo	Yang Yu
September 12th	China	The delegation to Japan from Fujian Province	
October 25th	Vietnam	The ambassador to Japan	Nguyen Quoc Cuong
October 29th	India	Prime Minister	Narendra Modi
November 2nd	Hong Kong	Chief Executive of Hong Kong	Carrie Lam Cheng Yuet-ngor
November 6th	Turkey	Minister of Foreign Affairs	Mevlüt Çavuşoğlu
November 19th	Nepal	Minister of Foreign Affairs	Pradeep Kumar Gyawali

November 21st	Arab countries	The delegation of Arab countries	
November 26th	Russia	A member of Federation Council	Viktor Ozerov
November 28th	India	The ambassador to Japan	Sujan Romeshchandra Chinoy
December 21th	Russia	First Deputy Chairman of the State Duma of Russia	Aleksandr Dmitrievich Zhukov
December 28th	Turkey	The ambassador to Japan	Hasan Murat Mercan

2019 (As the Secretary-General)

January 30th	Qatar	Emir	Tamim Bin Hamad Al-Thani
February 12th	India	The ambassador to Japan	Sanjay Kumar Verma
February 20th	China	The chairperson of Chinese People's Association for Friendship with Foreign Countries	Li Xiaolin
March 4th	China	The delegation of the travel bureau of Dalian, China	
March 4th	Myammar	Vice-Chairperson of National League for Democracy	Zaw Myint Maung
March 6th	Mongolia	The ambassador to Japan	Dambadarjaa Batjargal
March 13th	Laos	Head of Central Committee for Organization and Personnel, Lao People's Revolutionary Party	Chansy Phosikham
March 14th	South Korea	The delegation of The Federation of Korean Industries	
April 11th	China	The deputy director of International Liaison Department of the Chinese Communist Party	Qian Hongshan
April 11th	South Korea	The ambassador to Japan	Lee Su-hoon
May 15th	ASEAN	Secretary-General	Lim Jock Hoi
May 20th	Qatar	The ambassador to Japan	Hassan Bin Mohammed Rafei Al-Emadi
May 27th	South Korea	The ambassador to Japan	Nam Gwan-pyo
May 30th	Turkmenistan	President	Gurbanguly Berdimuhamedow

May 31st	Turkey	The ambassador to Japan	Hasan Murat Mercan
June 5th	China	The ambassador to Japan	Kong Xuanyou
June 6th	China	A member of the Politburo of the Communist Party of China	Cai Qi
July 1st	Turkey	President	Recep Tayyip Erdoğan
August 2nd	Nepal	The ambassador to Japan	Prativa Rana
August 5th	Vietnam	Chairperson of the Office of the Government	Mai Tien Dung
September 19th	ASEAN	Secretary-General	Lim Jock Hoi
September 24th	China	Vice-Chairperson of China Association for International exchange	Liu Hongcai
October 23rd	China	Vice President	Wang Qishan
October 25th	Kyrgyzstan	Minister of Foreign Affairs	Chingiz Aidarbekov
October 29th	Mexico	The ambassador to Japan	Melba María Pría Olavarrieta
November 15th	South Korea	The delegation of The Federation of Korean Industries	
November 29th	Uzbekistan	A former ambassador to Japan	Mirsobit Ochilov
December 5th	China	Communist Party Secretary of Shandong Province	Liu Jiayi
December 12th	Indonesia	Minister for Energy and Mineral Resources and the ambassador to Japan	Arifin Tasrif
December 17th	Venezuela	The ambassador to Japan	Seiko Luis Ishikawa Kobayashi
2020 (as the Secretary-General)			
September 29th	Turkmenistan	The ambassador to Japan	Gurbanmammet Elyasov
October 21st	Mongolia	The ambassador to Japan	Dambadarjaa Batjargal
November 18th	Qatar	The ambassador to Japan	Hassan Bin Mohammed Rafei Al-Emadi

The record of Nikai's foreign visits as the Secretary-General

2016		
September 8th - September 10th	Vietnam	Nguyen Phu Trong, the Secretary-General of Communist Party of Vietnam
		Nguyen Xuan Phuc, Prime Minister
		Nguyen The Kim Ngân, Chairperson of the National Assembly of Vietnam
November 2nd - November 4th	India	Narendra Modi, Prime Minister
		Rajnath Singh, Minister of Home Affairs
2017		
April 29th - May 4th	Fiji Tonga United States	To talk with high officials
May 13th - May 16th	China Beijing	To attend the "International Cooperation Forum of Belt and Road Initiative"
June 10th - June 13th	South Korea Mokpo, Seoul	To talk with high officials
July 18th - July 22nd	United States Washington D.C. New York	To attend the "U.N. Special session concerning water and disaster" To talk with high officials
December 24th - December 29th	China Xiamen, Wuyi Mountains Fuzhou, Beijing	To attend the "7th exchange conference of the ruling parties of Japan and China" To talk with high officials
2018		
April 26th - May 4th	Russia Turkey	To attend the "General assembly of Japan-Russia forum" To talk with high officials as the representative of LDP
May 25th - May 29th	China Dalian, Chengdu	To attend the "Sichuan earthquake 10th anniversary forum of disaster-prevention" as the representetive of LDP
August 29th - September 1st	China	To attend the "ceremony for the projects concerning the 40th anniversary of the re-establishment of diplomatic between Japan and China" as the representative of LDP
2019		
April 24th - April 29th	China Beijing, Shanghai	To attend the "International Cooperation Forum of Belt and Road Initiative"
2020		
January 11th - January 14th	Vietnam	To meet with high officials and visit as the representative of LDP concerning the exchanges by the party staffs

3. The testimony of Nakamura Eizo, the president of Wakayama Broadcasting System—Nikai's great contribution to his home, Wakayama

(1) A politician and his love for his home

Recently, under the single-seat constituency system, the number of candidates who run from a constituency which is not his hometown has been increasing bit by bit. However, under the multiple-seat constituency system in the past, the constituency and hometown of a candidate were the same in most cases. There were some politicians who run from the hometown of their wives, but these cases were rare.

Under the multiple-seat constituency system, candidates competed on the quality and quantity of their love for their hometown. Voters focused on them as well, and those who had contributed to their hometown the most won the election. The depth of love for the hometown, as well as the quality and quantity of the contribution to it were the most important factor for the result of elections.

The representative politician in the period of the multiple-seat constituency system was Tanaka Kakuei. His constituency was Echigo (the No. 3 constituency in Niigata), a snowy region. Tanaka passionately loved Echigo and devoted himself to improve the lives of the people there. I'm sure no one can surpass him in the love for his hometown and the energetic efforts for the development of it.

Nikai's mentor is Tanaka Kakuei. He inherited from Tanaka the sound conservative thoughts that a politician has a responsibility to love his hometown, care for the people, improve the lives of the people, especially those who aren't fortunate, and create a peaceful world.

Tanaka made efforts for the development of Echigo and it was a natural task of a politician. However, media people in Tokyo never tried to understand Tanaka properly but perverted his intention and criticized that he gave priority to the interest of his home.

Nikai also has made efforts for the development of his home,

Wakayama, fairly and impartially so that they don't invite malicious perversion of media people in Tokyo.

Tanaka was a genius of coordinating interests and was capable of doing things naturally and harmoniously. Nevertheless, he was criticized by media. Nikai is a genius of adjusting interests as well, but he has acted cautiously in order not to be misunderstood; he has always acted cautiously and kept the fair attitude.

After serving as a member of Wakayama Prefecture assembly for two terms, Nikai became a member of the Lower House and has been making efforts for the development of Wakayama, his home province, and improving the well-being of the people there for forty-five years. He has been devoting himself for the development of his home region while paying attention to the balance with other provinces. Nikai is the greatest politician with regard to the depth of love for his home.

(2) Nikai's achievements in his home for forty-five years

In wakayama, there is an excellent journalist whom I respect, and he is my closest friend as well: Nakamura Eizo, the president of Wakayama Broadcasting System. Nakamura is a great intellectual and a living encyclopedia of Wakayama. When I collect information about Wakayama, I have always depended on him. Thus, the most of my knowledge about Wakayama Prefecture has come from him.

Responding to my request, Mr. Nakamura created a note about "the achievements of Nikai Toshihiro, a politician, in his home; a good friend is a great blessing indeed. Here I quote it.

When one looks back the political experience of Mr. Nikai Toshihiro, who served as a member of the prefectural assembly for eight years (two terms) and as a member of the Diet for thirty-seven years (twelve terms), he finds that Mr. Nikai's political ideal has been "with the home province", and the origin of his policies have been the "balanced development of the national land".

Here I (Nakamura) organize and list up the matters concerning the home province of Mr. Nikai.

❶ Development and improvement of traffic system

Specifically in the viewpoint of geography, in order to revive Wakayama, which deviates from the main axis line of the national land, i.e. the Tokaido Belt region, "developing traffic system of land, sea, and air" that would connect Wakayama to the axis line has been the most important issue.

[Land traffic]

* The inclusion of the entire construction plan of an expressway that would run around Kii Peninsula to the development plan of the government

* The development of roads, including Keinawa Expressway that connects Osaka and Nagoya via Wakayama Prefecture and Nara

* The extension of JR Super Express "Kuroshio" to Shin-Osaka station and connection to Shinkansen

[Air traffic]

* The construction of Kansai International Airport, the air gateway of Kansai area

* The improvement of Nanki Shirahama Airport to enable taking off and landing of jet airliners; Extending its 1,200 meter runway which only propeller aircrafts could take off and land to 1,800 - 2,000 meter runway which jet airlines also could take off and land

[Sea traffic]

* The improvement of important ports and bays, including Singuu Port of Hidaka Bay (Gobo city) and Wakayama Shimotsu port

❷ Projects concerning disaster-prevention and disaster-reduction

Though disaster-prevention and disaster-reduction can be categorized as a part of "national resilience", they are based on his own experiences such as "7/18 flood disaster" and "Kano River Typhoon".

He realized the improvement of measures against tsunami and policies for disaster-prevention

Further efforts for risk management, including Covid-19 catastrophe, is expected in the future.

❸ Sightseeing projects and international exchanges in Wakayama

Mr. Nikai, who always says, "the tourism resources of an area rest even in a leaf. It is up to the efforts of the people whether it can be discovered and improved", has been engaged in the development of the tourism resources of his home province. In particular, he has made a lot of achievements, such as the ones below.

* While engaging in peace and friendship diplomatic activities, he has used them to get publicity for the local tourism resources. For example, he invited President Gül of Turkey to Kushimoto town and held the memorial service for the victims of the sea accident of Ertugrul Firkateyni, a battleship of turkey, in which more than 600 crews died.

* Following the establishment of "World Tsunami Awareness Day", he held "World High School Students Summit", to which high school students of foreign countries were invited to study about disaster-prevention, in various places including Wakayama. And he initiated a study session in the "Inamura-no-Hi no Yakata (House of Fire of Shock)" of Hamaguchi Goryo.

* He deployed a peace and friendship diplomatic activity of Lotus Road via Oga Lotus and used it to get publicity for the sightseeing in his home province.

❹ Efforts for solving the issues of the people and saving the disadvantaged people

* While Taiji, a town of whales, suffered hardship after commercial whale hunting was banned, he made efforts to resume it.

* As damages by wild animals spread, he made efforts to get rid of

them and familiarize gibier cuisine.

* For the physically challenged people who are using wheelchair, he promoted the barrier-free in public spaces such as JR stations.

* He devoted himself to pass the "Act on the Promotion of the Elimination of Buraku Discrimination"

Nakamura showed us specifically a part of political achievements of Nikai in his home province which aren't known to many people.

It is important to note that they are not just what Nikai has done only for Wakayama, his home province. Nikai knows well that the issues in Wakayama are not only what he should solve especially for his own constituency, but also the issues of the whole nation. Thus, he has taken the voice of the people in his home province as the voice of the entire Japanese people, formulated policies for the entire Japan, and set them into action. Nikai has never brought benefits only to his home.

The ones who know such kind of political achievements of Nikai better than anyone else are the people of Wakayama. Though extremely busy, he has made time as much as possible to visit his home province and listen to each one of ordinary people carefully. In my view, it is why he has been able to realize policies which emphasize the lives of the people and care for them.

Nikai's love for his home is deep, high, broad, and pure.

I have called Nikai the "saint of Kisyu" in my mind; I have been thinking that Nikai parallels, or surpasses, Hanaoka Seisyu, Hamaguchi Goryo, and Minakata Kumagusu in his love for home, and is a great figure who can be called the "saint of Kisyu".

4. The testimony of Kado Hirofumi—Learning from Nikai's deep love for his home

(1) Nikai's deep love for his home described by his disciple

Kado Hirofumi, a member of the Lower House and the LDP branch chief of Wakayama No.1 constituency, is one of the disciples of Nikai. His father is a famous local politician who, after serving as an official of LDP's Wakayama Prefecture branch, served as a member of the prefectural assembly for forty years (ten terms) and is the closest friend of Nikai, who was his comrade as a member of the prefectural assembly, throughout his lifetime. In addition, Nikai acted as the go-between in Hirofumi's wedding.

After graduating from Wakayama University, Kado worked as a businessman for twenty-three years and as the manager of a company run by Matsushita Konosuke, whom he respects. After that, he decided to serve as a politician, run for the Lower House election of 2012, and became a member of it. Now he is active as one of the closest aids of Nikai and accompanies him in his activities in Wakayama very often.

I heard from Kado about how deep Nikai's love for his home is. Kado talked as follows.

(2) The testimony of Kado Hirofumi

Mr. Nikai became a member of Wakayama prefectural assembly in 1975 and, after serving for eight years (two terms), proceeded to the Lower House and has served as its member for thirty-seven years. For forty-five years in total, he has devoted himself to the development of Wakayama Prefecture.

Before that, he worked as a secretary of Mr. Shindo Saburo, a member of the Lower House in Shizuoka Prefecture, but all the while he loved Wakayama, was concerned about Wakayama, and worked for Wakayama.

Now I am working near Mr. Nikai, and I can say with absolute certainty that his depth of love and enthusiasm for his home is outstanding. He always thinks, "I want to improve my home province anyway", "I want to make those who live there richer and happier", and "what can I do for it?" and has made efforts for them. He is made of the love for his home place from head to toe, and I cannot come close to him.

Even now, Mr. Nikai returns to Wakayama every week. Almost no veteran Diet members of LDP, who have won the election ten, eleven, or twelve times, return to their constituency as often as Mr. Nikai does. Veteran Diet members hold a strong base in their constituency and many of them spend Saturdays and Sundays in Tokyo, but Mr. Nikai is different.

He returns to Wakayama not only in election campaign periods but every weekend, meets with the people there, and listens to their voices. And when disaster occurs, he quickly visits the affected areas.

Since he became a member of the Lower House thirty-seven years ago, Mr. Nikai has continued to live like this and returns to Wakayama almost every week even now. This pattern of activity has never changed, and we junior fellows have to emulate it.

The biggest contribution of Mr. Nikai to Wakayama Prefecture is the construction of the expressway that runs around Kii Peninsula. He has made efforts for it for forty years and by now the framework has been made. Though it will take five to ten years until it fully opens, those who live in Kii Peninsula feel delight. Mr. Nikai has been tackling this big project which takes decades and made efforts for it.

When Mr. Nikai came up with his plan for the construction of the expressway that would run around Kii Peninsula forty-five years ago, some ridiculed him as a big mouth. However, he has continued his efforts with persistence.

When this expressway opens, Kii Peninsula will make a great leap forward.

Mr. Nikai made a great contribution to the construction and improvement of Kansai International Airport (Kankuu) as well. The airport is located off the Senshu shore at the south part of Osaka Prefecture, but for the people of Wakayama, "Kankuu" is "Wakayama Airport". And Mr. Nikai worked hard since his youth to promote the construction of an airport and enhance its function.

Mr. Nikai worked hard for the enhancement and improvement of Nanki Shirahama Airport as well. Now three daily flights to Tokyo are operated, and they are the result of Mr. Nikai's activities.

Mr. Nikai has contributed to the improvement of ports and harbors as well. Hidaka Bay is located in the home province of him and if a road between the harbor and the expressway opens, it will develop further, and the lives of the people will be improved.

The main port in Wakayama is "Wakayama Shimotsu Port". If Osaka Bay, Kobe Port, and Wakayama Shimotsu Port are operated in an integrated way, the ports and harbors of Kansai area will develop further too.

Mount Koya and Kumano Kodo are the two representative tourism resources of Wakayama Prefecture and will attract many foreign tourists again once Covid-19 catastrophe calms down. In addition, when the improvement of road networks is completed, the number of tourists will increase.

Among the social contributions by Mr. Nikai, the establishment of "World Tsunami Awareness Day: November 5th" in U.N. is really significant. It was realized by his efforts. Also, Nikai made known to the world the "Fire of Shock" by Hamaguchi Goryo, a great figure born in Wakayama. Thus, the events concerning the "World Tsunami Awareness Day" has been held not only in Japan but all over the world.

Mr. Nikai has contributed to Wakayama in cultural and academic aspects as well. He devoted himself to educational campaigns to spread the great achievements of Hanaoka Seisyu, the "genius of medicine", and Minakata Kumagusu, the "giant of intellect", both born in Wakayama.

Furthermore, Mr. Nikai has been engaged in cultural activities to spread Oga Lotus throughout the world. He exchanged Oga Lotus for Vietnamese Lotus and it was planted in Kinokawa city. And Prime Minister Phúc of Vietnam visited Kinokawa for the exchange via Lotus. And recently, Mr. Nikai visited the home of Prime Minister Phúc along with the delegate consisting of 1,000 persons. He has performed such international exchanges for friendship and goodwill based in Wakayama Prefecture.

The exchanges between Wakayama and China and Korea are frequently performed as well and they are also the result of Mr. Nikai's efforts.

We junior fellows will exert ourselves to come close to Mr. Nikai's deep love for his home. The people of Wakayama are proud of Mr. Nikai.

5. The testimony of Tsuruho Yosuke, a member of the Upper House—The origin of "Nikai-ism" with which he always renders a service for others

(1) Tsuruho Yosuke, LDP's political leader and powerful ace

Tsuruho Yosuke is a member of the Upper House from Wakayama Prefecture and has more than twenty years' experience in the Diet. After serving as a secretary of a politician, he won the Upper House election in 1998 at thirty-one, the youngest at that time. He is intelligent, with cheerful and pleasant personality, and full of love for his home, which he inherited from Nikai.

Though he is a figure with high potential who can be the top leader of Japanese politics and lead Japan, Tsuruho always behaves humbly; he thinks that it is his mission from heaven to render a service for Nikai as his prime disciple. Saying in an Aristotle way, Tsuruho is an excellent orthodox politician who has the same excellence in ethic and intelligence as Nikai.

About twenty years ago, when Liberal Democratic Party and New Conservative Party merged on an equal footing, Nikai took measures for his allies of NCP to join traditional factions of LDP to ensure their future. Thanks to this warm-heartedness of Nikai, his allies of NCP could find an arena of activities and make a leap forward. As a result, Nikai group reduced to just two members: Nikai himself and Tsuruho.

Nikai and Tsuruho are a mentor and a disciple, as well as allies, with inseparable relations; it is close to parent and child relationship.

In fact, the fathers of Nikai and Tsuruho were relatives and both families share the same ancestors. Tsuruho is a "person who knows most often says least" type of politician and I think he has the potential to be a top leader of the political world of Japan.

Here I quote the testimony of Tsuruho Yousuke.

(2) The testimony of Tsuruho Yosuke

When I run for the Upper House election for the first time about twenty years ago, though I wasn't a member of LDP then, Mr. Nikai came to support me and said to the voters, "Have you ever seen any Upper House member of LDP? If so, please raise your hand". At first, I wondered why he said so, but then he continued, "you should not choose as the representative of the area those who think they need not return to their home province". Hearing this, the audience applauded heartily. Mr. Nikai is a politician who cares for his home province.

Even now, Mr. Nikai frequently returns to Wakayama. Because such a great senior colleague as him has kept returning to his home province for more than thirty years, we junior fellows have to return to our home province as well. Some time ago, I was commended by ANA (All Nippon Airways) because I frequently use its flights and has accumulated a lot of frequent flier mileage. I follow an example set by Mr. Nikai and go back and forth between Wakayama and Tokyo as often as possible.

Mr. Nikai is a person full of ideas. When a voter visits him to make petitions, it's Mr. Nikai who teaches how to make petitions to him. Some voters might be bewildered, but they would find out that he is correct in the end.

When looking at the activities of Mr. Nikai as a politician, it seems that they are influenced by Mr. Nikai Syuntaro (a former member of Wakayama prefectural assembly), his father. Mr. Nikai Syuntaro was a distant relative of my father, and according to my father, Mr. Nikai Syuntaro was a great politician who closely cooperated with local people, run around his home province with his face tanning, and acted for ordinary people.

There is an area called Nada near Gobo city, and a bronze statue of Mr. Nikai Syuntaro stands there.

In the past, a land improvement project was implemented in Nada and a wonderful garden was constructed. Thus, local people who respected him constructed the statue; Mr. Nikai Syuntaro was such a great figure who earned the esteem of them.

Mr. Nikai Toshihiro is a politician of few words. It might be a rare case, for majority of politicians are voluble. So he has been misunderstood sometimes. However, the amazing thing about him is that he never defends himself; Mr. Nikai is such a grand person.

Because of his reticence, Mr. Nikai has always a lot of options. I, too, have come to understand the merit of being reticent in attaining experience. If one saves his breath, he listens carefully. And never fail to do what he promised. This is Mr. Nikai's style.

Mr. Nikai values highly the interaction with people; he is a genius of it. And in my view, this is greatly due to the influence of his father, Mr. Nikai Syuntaro. According to my father, Mr. Nikai Syuntaro also valued highly the interaction. Mr. Nikai Toshihiro has stuck to the way of living "Those who come are welcome, those who leave are not regretted", and I think it is what he inherited from his father.

Once, during the period of "Showa great merger of municipalities", the head of Kitayama, a village surrounded by Mie and Nara Prefecture as an enclave, visited Mr. Nikai and said, "Mr. Nikai, we are planning to leave Wakayama and join Mie or Nara because we don't want to be an enclave any longer. How do you think?" Hearing this, Mr. Nikai scolded loudly, "If you move to other prefectures, you don't need to visit me!" Mr. Nikai kept the attitude of "Those who come are welcome, those who leave are not regretted", and Kitayama has been belonging to Wakayama

Prefecture up to now.

Mr. Nikai has made a lot of rules about his conduct; there are quite a few of small rules and he lives complying with them. In addition, his life is highly principled. I have worked closely with him for a long time, so I know his rules and communicate them to junior Diet members. They include a lot of basic rules important for a politician.

At one point, our group had only two Diet members, Mr. Nikai and me, but it was because Mr. Nikai gave consideration to the future of other members and provided them ways to survive. In this way, each member of our group except me could gain his position. Mr. Nikai never cared about the decreasing number of his own group but gave advice to them putting their future first. As such, Mr. Nikai always cares for others and is concerned about their future.

In the end, we returned to LDP through the merger of LDP and NCP, and it might be because Mr. Nikai gave consideration to my future. Though Mr. Nikai said nothing about it, I think it was painful for him to return to LDP. However, after returning LDP, he began a great leap forward.

After Prime Minister Abe resigned this time, some member of Nikai faction said that it should field a candidate in the LDP presidential election. This opinion seemed natural considering the presence and accomplishments of our faction. But I thought that Mr. Nikai would never aim to be the president of LDP, so I advised those who wanted to encourage him to run for the election not to beat the air. It seemed to me that Mr. Nikai wanted only to contribute to the society as the Secretary-General of LDP, and didn't think about anything above it, that is, the position of Prime Minister.

Mr. Nikai is a politician who always cares for his home province, gives consideration to ordinary people, especially the unfortunate ones, and lives with them.

I follow Mr. Nikai as a good example and make efforts every day to come as close to him as possible.

6. A life of benevolence which Nikai's great parents lived— A spirit Nikai inherited from his parents

Nikai speaks little; including his closest family member, Nikai clan is all reticent ladies and gentlemen.

Among them, I have heard about the parents of Nikai sometimes; they were greatly respected by local people. The ancestors of Nikai's mother were all physicians and Nikai's mother herself was an excellent doctor who graduated from Tokyo Women's Medical School (currently known as Tokyo Women's Medical University). She was a female doctor who made a great contribution to the local healthcare of Wakayama Prefecture and saved the lives of local people. They profoundly thanked Dr. Nikai Kikue and respected her.

On the other hand, Nikai's father was a local politician who was greatly respected and adored by local people. He was humble and known as a person of integrity.

Both of his parents worked tirelessly to improve people's lives.

In the past, I learned about Nikai's parents mainly from the testimonies of those who knew them, for I could find almost no documents which described their lives exactly. However, when I began to write this book, a staff of Higashi Nippon International University, which I belong to, provided me with a document via his friend in Wakayama. The title of the document is 'A record of funeral of Mrs. Nikai Kikue', which was edited and published at the first anniversary of her death. At the same time, the ceremony of seventeenth anniversary of Nikai Syuntaro's death was held, and a quote from 'Memory of late Mr. Nikai Syuntaro', which had been published on October 4th 1975, was included in the document.

On the first page of 'A record of funeral of Mrs. Nikai Kikue' is a photo of Nikai Syuntaro and Kikue, which was taken in Tokyo on May 1971, when Nikai Syuntaro was decorated. In the photo, they are a beautiful old couple with dignity.

The memorial service of Mrs. Nikai was held at Gobo municipal gymnasium in Wakayama prefecture on July 29th 1990. Kariya Shiro, the governor of Wakayama Prefecture, acted as the head of the funeral committee. And in the list of the attendees were the names of Okuda Keiwa (Minister of Home Affairs and Chairperson of the National Public Safety Commission), Sato Megumu (the chief of Keisei-kai), Nakanishi Keisuke (a member of the Lower House), Nonaka Hiromu (the same), Ibuki Bunmei (the same), Matsuda Iwao (the same), and Okazima Masayuki (the same). They were all politicians with whom I had been acquainted.

Twenty-eight thousand people gathered at the funeral of Mrs. Nikai and prayed for her. This fact shows the greatness of Mrs. Nikai who was deeply respected by the people of not only Wakayama but all over Japan.

At the funeral, some of the condolence telegrams were read. Among them were the ones from Kaifu Toshiki, the president of Liberal Democratic Party and Prime Minister, Kanemaru Shin, a member of the Lower House and the chairperson of Keisei-kai, and Takeshita Noboru, the former Prime Minister. It signifies the presence of Mrs. Nikai, as well as that of Representative Nikai Toshihiro, her son.

At the first part of the document, "The life of Mrs. Nikai Kikue" is recorded. It is a precious record, so I quote its whole text here.

"The life of Mrs. Nikai Kikue"

Mrs. Nikai Kikue was born in Hidaka-gun Ryujin-mura Tonohara on November 1st of Meiji 32 (1899), as the third daughter of Dr. Furukubo Ryosuke and Sawa.

She graduated from Tomisato elementary school, Iwata elementary school, and Kurusugawa higher-elementary school, then the former Tanabe women's high school. And in Taisho 8 (1919), she temporarily worked as an assistant teacher of Hioki elementary school, but following his father's wish that she would succeed him as a doctor, proceeded to Tokyo women's school, currently known as Tokyo Women's Medical University, in Taisho

9 (1920). There she studied under Yoshioka Yayoi, the founder of Tokyo Women's Medical School and pioneer of female doctors. Then, during the period of Kanto Great Earthquake which occurred in Taisho 12 (1923), she studied hard as one of the female medical students, which were rare at that time, obtained a medical license in the next year, and opened her clinic in Shinmachi area of Gobo city.

From Taisho to Showa era, she was respected by many patients and trusted as "Doctor Kokubo" and "Miss Doctor".

Later, she married late Nikai Syuntaro, a former member of Wakayama prefectural assembly, and was blessed with two sons and two daughters.

Local people know well that she grew her children as a mother, worked hard as a doctor, and supported election campaigns as a wife, and later as a mother, for a long time.

After World War II, she contributed for a long time to the local medical service mainly as a doctor of Yuasa public health center of Wakayama Prefecture.

Mrs. Nikai Kikue lived her life of ninety years, through the ages of Meiji, Taisho, Showa, and Heisei, as a woman of Meiji. She rests peacefully now, and we imagine she is smiling contentedly, thinking "no regret for my life" and "it's all thanks to you", which she repeated during her hospital stay.

We, along with the attendees, wish she rests eternally peacefully.

In 'A record of funeral of Mrs. Nikai Kikue', a text from 'The Memory' which was published by "The group of persons who commemorate Mr. Nikai Syuntaro" is included. And the calligrapher who wrote the title was Yamaguchi Kikuichiro, who had served as the speaker of the Lower House.

Syoji Keijiro, a member of the Lower House who read a condolence speech at the funeral of Nikai Syuntaro, spoke as follows. Here I quote its whole text.

A condolence speech by Syoji Keijiro

I solemnly give my condolence speech in front of the soul of late Nikai Syuntaro, with The Order of the Rising Sun, Gold and Silver Rays.

Mr. Nikai, you were born in Mimai village of Nishimuro District in Meiji 33 (1900), became a teacher at a young age, and crossed the Pacific more than ten times as a crew on foreign routes. Then, you aspired to be a politician and became a manager of Gobo branch of Kii-shinpo newspaper as a first step.

Later, you established a local paper in Gobo and managed the company, while you got acquainted with Koike Ushinosuke and made a strategic move toward the political circle of Wakayama. You run for the by-election of the prefectural assembly in Showa 13 (1938) and won it at an age of thirty-eight. By the way, according to your wishes, your son, Toshihiro, became a member of the prefectural assembly at an age of thirty-six, two years younger than you when you had won the election. You must be delighted by this.

After that, you acted as a member of the prefectural assembly, the chief of Inahara village, and the president of Gobo Zosen, one of the largest companies in Hidaka area. And following the purge after World War II, you became a member of the prefectural assembly in Showa 34 (1959) again and served as the chairperson of civil engineering committee, the chairperson of agriculture and forestry committee, and the chief of Gobo branch of LDP Wakayama during the eight years until Showa 42 (1967).

Mr. Nikai, in the seventeen years during and after the War, you made innumerable achievements as a member of the prefectural assembly. Among them, especially important was that you realized the merger of three weirs, Wakano, Noguchi, and Rokugo. Having overcome various difficulties during the War, the long-waited strong integrated weir was completed in Showa 19 (1944) after three years of efforts. Thus, you passed down an irrigation system which could water thousands acres of Hidaka plain for a thousand years.

In addition, when I aspired to be a politician, you invited the then Minister of Agriculture Fukuda Takeo to Gobo to realize the construction of irrigation system in Nada town and Route 42.

Mr. Nikai, you are a great person beloved by people. Needless to say, many people whom you cared for adored your virtue. I, too, had you as the instructor of politics and your speech attracted the audience in my election campaigns.

Furthermore, though you experienced an extreme hardship during the purge after the War, you lived a carefree life, endowed with splendid and distinctive character. And recently, your son succeeded you as a politician, which was your long-time wish. We hoped to learn from you as the elder of political circle of Kisyu, but, just as a proverb says, "happy events tend to be accompanied by problems", you suddenly, at the same time peacefully, passed away. We truly regret it.

Here I praise your antemortem achievements, commemorate your virtue, and thank you for innumerable obligations I owe to you. I pray sincerely for the repose of your soul and end my condolence speech.

October 7th Showa 50 (1975)

(a member of the Lower House)

At the funeral of Mr. Nikai Syuntaro, a representative of the governor of Wakayama Prefecture, Diet members from Wakayama, and many of the prefectural assembly members attended and politicians who represented Wakayama made their condolence speech. Among them was Hayakawa Takashi, a member of the Lower House and a powerful politician who was active in the central political circle of Japan then. I met with Hayakawa several times.

A condolence speech by Machida Yoshitomo, a member of the prefectural assembly and one of closest friends of Mr. Nikai, described plangently how great he had been. At the same time, Machida spoke about the high hopes the people of Wakayama had for Mr. Nikai's elder son, Toshihiro. Here I quote the whole text of it.

A condolence speech by Machida Yoshitomo

Autumn, when leaves fell to ground, makes a man feel lonely, however subtle it is. Beyond that, while we felt pain and sadness at the death of Governor Ohashi, we lost our friend Mr. Nikai Syuntaro as well.

Ah, a life is filled with sadness. Here I stand in front of your soul, express my sincere condolences, and bid an eternal farewell to you.

Thinking I can no longer call you "Mr. Nikai", I feel extreme sadness. Both you and I were born near Hiki river in Nishimuro District, you in Hisagi, I in Chikatsuyu. Besides, we were members of the prefectural assembly, both belonging to neutral group when the antagonism between Seiyu Party and Minsei Party was tense. And along with late Mr. Nishikawa Hiroshi and Mr. Ishikawa, we shared the food out of the same pan as allies. In addition, in the general election held in 1946 under the rule of GHQ, in which the entire Wakayama Prefecture was a single constituency, we run for it along with forty-eight other candidates with the young aspiration. After that, we both were purged, you as the head of a village, me as the leader of Yokusan Sounen group, and cried in a prison without bars. Then, on December 1946, we left from the world of politics in sorrow.

And when I was depurged first and run for four Lower House elections, you and your mother supported me both publicly and privately. It was an unforgettable joy for me and I have felt a great obligation to you.

Mr. Nikai.

I miss the days when we both became members of the prefectural assembly again after the war. Your eloquent and unique speech was known as "Nikai-tone", and you had an especially good memory which surprised me often. You visited Tokyo frequently and often cried out on the platform of the assembly to realize that irrigation system in Nada and a national road which passed through Yura; the achievements which were realized through your efforts, sincerity, and eloquent questions were really great. Now, the bronze statue of Mr. Hamaguchi, the first chairperson of the prefectural assembly, stands in front of the north wing of the prefectural office building, and it was achieved by your questions against the then Governor Ono. Whenever I see the statue, I will recall you.

When one thinks his friend is still alive on the same horizon, he will not call to mind, think of, and recall this friend. Now that you have passed away and I can no longer see you, all the memories of the past revive beautifully in my mind. Mr. Nikai, whenever I see that statue you left behind, I will never fail to pray for you. Now I feel the pain and sorrow of losing my closest friend with whom I could talk about the assembly before the war.

However, the sprinkler in Nada will move eternally showing your enthusiasm and achievements. And the national road via Yura and the river behind the station will remain along with the history. Above all, your elder son Toshihiro won the fierce battle in the election and debuted in the assembly as a star rookie. Though this is due to the ability of him and the power of his friends and supporters, I believe your virtue contributed to it as well. It is not exaggerating to say that you were fortunate because you could grow a good successor while you were alive. I, too, have a high hope and dream for his future and will support him as much as possible. I believe that nothing other than this word and this feeling of mine can be the farewell gift to repay your friendship and mourn your death.

Nikai Toshihiro is a man of fine character.

So, at the last of my speech, I regret the eternal farewell and, in my deepest sorrow, thank you for your friendship and pray for the repose of your soul.

May your soul come and take it.

October 7th 1975

(A member of the prefectural assembly and the representative of the friends)

Nikai Toshihiro devoted himself to realize "World Tsunami Awareness Day: November 5th"(that is the day of the "Fire of Shock", the achievement by Hamaguchi Goryo), and the speech showed that it was his father Syuntaro who had realized the construction of the statue of Hamaguchi Goryo in front of the prefectural office North wing. The project of passing down Hamaguchi Goryo's great accomplishment was done by Syuntaro and Toshihiro, a father and his son.

The true source of Nikai's spirit as a politician is his father Mr. Syuntaro and his mother Mrs. Kikue. Their spirits were passed down to Toshihiro and turned into his present spirit.

The parents and their son can be called the "falcons of Kisyu". Not only the father or the mother, but they both. Toshihiro inherited Buddha's integrity from his father and kindness of Holy Mother from his mother.

It was Heinrich Heine, a German poet, who said "Great genius takes shape by contact with another great genius", and Nikai Toshihiro's genius took shape by contact with his parents. Thus, the origin of Nikai Toshihiro is his parents, both of whom were respected by everyone like saints.

Nikai Toshihiro inherited from his parents a spirit of noble service to work for everyone and proceeded to the world of politics, and this is the origin of his spirit.

After graduating a university, Nikai became a secretary of Endo Saburo, a Diet member whose constituency was Shizuoka No.2 in the period of multiple-seat electoral system. At first, he had hoped to work as a secretary of Esaki Masumi (the father of Esaki Tetsuma, a member of the Lower House), a powerful politician of Aichi Prefecture, but his wish wasn't realized, so he became a secretary of Endo, who was intimate with Esaki. Endo was a great politician as well. Endo had a close relation with Syuntaro. Nikai's father entrusted his son to Endo. Nikai was adored and loved by people in Shizuoka No.2 constituency as Endo's excellent secretary.

By the way, my home province is Ito, Shizuoka Prefecture, and Ito was the constituency of Endo. Even now, those who have been involved in the political community of Izu Peninsula for a long time remember Nikai Toshihiro as an excellent and energetic secretary. And an old supporter of Endo said to me, "Mr. Nikai was an outstanding secretary. He listened to petitions sincerely and he was superior to an ordinary minister in his faculty.

I have heard voices of people like, "I owe a lot of obligations to Mr. Nikai", in various places of Shizuoka; Nikai was deeply respected by the people in Shizuoka No.2 constituency. Though he could have succeeded Endo as a Diet member, Nikai returned to his home province, became a member of the prefectural assembly and later a member of the Diet. Nikai trained himself as a politician under Endo in determination to work for Wakayama in the future.

Through the forty-five years as a politician, eight years as a member of the prefectural assembly and thirty-seven years as a member of the Lower House, Nikai has worked for the world peace, the happiness of humankind, the Japanese people, and the people in Wakayama, with an energetic spirit of service. And now, he has become a great figure who is said to be the most powerful in the political world of Japan.

Presently, Nikai is taking an inventory of his life as a politician; he is tackling great challenges of both international and domestic politics with his genius political ability. And I hope he will continue to work for ten more years.

The aim of Nikai as a politician is the realization of eternal peace and the resilience of human society. During these ten years, Nikai has made efforts for national resilience, but the resilience of human society as a whole, including not only social infrastructure but thoughts and culture, will be important in the future. Resilience means to construct a society which is strong, flexible, and sustainable. I hope Nikai continues to work at least for ten more years, until 2030s, for eternal peace and the resilience of human society.

Chapter 5

A challenge for new issues—For eternal peace and the resilience of human society

Threefold the stride of "Time", from first to last!
Loitering slow, the Future creepeth —
Arrow-swift, the Present sweepeth —
And motionless forever stands the Past.——*Schiller*

1. "Nikai-ism" shown in recent words and deeds of Secretary-General Nikai

Though Secretary-General Nikai is reticent, he has begun to speak up recently; he has come to speak "Nikai-ism", his political ideals. It is quite preferable. Among these utterances, there are three topics which attract attentions recently.

First is the relationship with China and South Korea, second is his assessment about Tanaka Kakuei, and third is the improvement of the management of the liaison meeting between the government and ruling parties.

(1) The relationship with China and South Korea

On November 13th 2020 (Friday), Nikai appeared on "Prime News" of BS-Fuji and replied to the questions by the newscaster calmly and politely. It was rare for Nikai, because the acting Secretary-General had usually appeared on TV shows on his behalf. The newscaster of "Prime News" seemed to despise China and South Korea, so he tried to have Nikai say something against these two countries. But Nikai wasn't deluded by it and spoke up his opinion without hesitation.

"We should get along with neighboring countries, for any country can never move away. So, friendship is important. The world is watching whether Japan is a country capable of befriending neighboring countries or not. For Japan to be respected, we have to show that it is a country which can be intimate with neighboring countries".

Recently, narrow-minded nationalism which regards China and South Korea with hostility has been spreading in Japan; more and more people fan the conflict with these two countries. Is it that a biased view toward China and Korea before World War II, when Japan colonized the two countries, is reviving among some of politicians and journalists? The pledge by the Japanese people after World War II, "we never wage a war again, never invade Asian countries again", faces a greater opposition now. Nikai is trying to mitigate such a trend.

As for China, the U.S. government is encouraging Asian countries to join the international coalition against it, and the encouragement to Japan has become quite intense. As a result, a dangerous trend has been spreading in Japan that, by the encouragement from U.S., it is involved in the coalition against China gradually. If we allow this trend to go on, the Japanese people will never be safe; Japan's future will be bleak if it comes into collision with China. In contrast, Nikai is devoting himself to the safety and prosperity of Japan.

Though Japan is an ally of U.S. in terms of its security, it heavily depends on China economically. Many companies have been expanding their business to China and manufacturing goods there. As anti-China atmosphere has grown in Japan, some of these companies are trying to retreat from China and move their operation into other Asian countries such as Vietnam, but it cannot be done soon and will take some time. China is still quite important as the "factory of the world", and many Japanese companies continues their operation in China. Thus, security is not the only important factor for a country and economic stability is also necessary.

Japan is an economic state; if Japan sees China with hostility, it will bring nothing but harm. Japan should exert its wisdom and ability to maintain the economic cooperation with China while keeping a friendly relationship with U.S. Furthermore, Japan must be engaged in active diplomatic activities and make efforts for the reconciliation between these two countries. This is "Nikai-ism".

If Japan follows the U.S. government, joins the international coalition against China and develops a hostile relationship with it, Japanese companies operating in China will not be guaranteed protection. Rather, those companies might face an enormous loss. Speaking in the extreme, if the Japanese government follows U.S and joins the coalition against China, it means abandoning Japanese companies operating in China. If it comes down to it, Japanese economy will fall into turmoil. Japanese economy might shrink drastically if it conforms with U.S. policies which is hostile to China. This does no good to Japan.

Japan has political and economic responsibility as the center of Asia; it bears responsibility to protect the peace in Asia and make it prosper economically. In order to secure its own national interest, Japan cannot support only U.S. in the U.S.-China conflict. Japan, the important great power in Asia, must execute a mission to act as a bridge between U.S. and China.

Secretary-General Nikai is a pacifist who believes Japan has important responsibility for the peace in Asia.

In this conflict between U.S. and China, if Japan stands on the side of U.S. only, it will not bring peace. Japan has to maintain friendly relationship not only with U.S. but also with China.

Recently, anti-China opinions gain strong momentum in LDP as well and those who view China with hostility are increasing among its Diet members. In addition, more politicians and journalists are advocating the coalition with U.S., Australia, U.K. and Taiwan against China. A militaristic trend gains momentum, too. A situation like this is extremely dangerous to Japan, a country of economy and peace.

Nikai is trying to stop this trend from expanding, to maintain and strengthen a peaceful and friendly relationship with not only U.S. but also with China. This is worth praise. Japanese people should support Nikai's pacifism and protect Japan, a state of peace, to the end.

Recently, I often read Chinese newspapers translated in Japanese and notice that their tone is changing subtly. In my view, while the Chinese government hopes a peaceful and friendly relationship with Japan, it increases a sense of caution gradually; in China, a view that Japan is becoming a base for the military operation of U.S. forces against China has gained momentum. Though the Chinese government strongly hopes to maintain and develop a peaceful and friendly relationship with Japan, people's feeling toward Japan is changing subtly. Especially after Covid-19 catastrophe, criticism in China against Japan becomes tenser.

If U.S. military forces should attack the mainland China, it will definitely strike back. Though the target of the People's Liberation Army will be U.S. bases in Japan, other places might be attacked if a war occurs between U.S. and China; big cities of Japan will inevitably be a target of an attack by atomic bomb. If so, Japan will be totally destroyed.

Japan should not depend on military forces. It must live as a country of peace, economy, culture, and science and technology.

Secretary-General Nikai also believe Japan should take this path.

Now, Japan faces crossroads as to whether it should go along with the anti-China policies of the U.S. government and survive with the military alliance with it, or it should maintain a friendly relationship with China as well. Meanwhile, Nikai makes efforts to direct Japan toward the simultaneous cooperation with U.S. and China.

I believe that Nikai is the true leader of the Japanese people who wish for peace; he devotes himself to maintain a peaceful and friendly relationship with China as well as U.S., so he can be called the guardian deity for the peace in Asia and the Japanese people.

The relationship with South Korea is important, too. Since Moon Jae-in became the President of South Korea, the former Abe Cabinet had taken a tough attitude toward it that Japan would not agree to hold discussion unless the Korean government changes its attitude. Japanese media also supported this attitude by the Abe administration.

However, Nikai has always argued, "We should get along with neighboring countries. The world is watching whether Japan is a country capable of befriending neighboring countries or not. If Japan fails to maintain the peaceful and friendly relationship with South Korea, it cannot be respected in the international community. In order to maintain the international credibility of Japan, we must protect the peaceful relationship with South Korea". I believe this attitude of Nikai is right and correct. Also, the Korean government also hopes to create a friendly relationship with the new administration led by Prime Minister Suga and has made efforts for it.

Korean newspapers are translated in Japanese as well, so we can read the opinions of the major Korean newspapers. When I read a Korean newspaper, I can understand that the Korean people and its government regard Japan as a quite important neighboring country. Though some have mixed feelings toward Japan because of the historical context, many strongly hope for the friendly cooperation relationship with Japan; even if there are differences of viewpoint between the governments of Japan and Korea, they wish to overcome these differences and establish the friendly relationship with Japan. Majority of Korean people, politicians, businesspersons, and ordinary people alike, strongly hope for the friendship with Japan.

However, the hardened attitude of the Japanese government toward Korea seems unchanged even after Suga became the new Prime Minister. I hope that the Suga Cabinet takes a more flexible attitude.

The present situation where South Korea committedly makes efforts to improve the relationship with Japan will not last forever, and I predict that it changes any time soon.

Some key persons in the Japan-Korea relationship whom I met in South Korea two years ago basically regarded the friendship between the two countries as quite important. The statue of a comfort woman near the Japanese embassy in Seoul has been a subject of the excessive coverage by Japanese media, but when I visited the actual place, it was placed at the roadside of the embassy and hard to spot; not a pedestrian stopped to look at it. In my view, the Korean people are not so anti-Japan as reported in Japanese and Korean media.

However, when Korean people feels that Japan completely ignores the Korea's initiative toward friendship with it, there will be a possibility the Japan-Korea relationship turns bad and the anti-Japanese sentiment of the Korean people flames up. It is not good prospect for Japan. The message from Korea that it hopes to remedy the friendship with Japan may be awkward a bit, but the Japanese government should not ignore it. Japan should regard it as a chance for the reconciliation and make use of it for the friendship between the two countries; it is a mature attitude in the international community.

Presently, it might be only Secretary-General Nikai, Kawamura Takeo, the secretary-general of the Japan–Korea Parliamentarians' Union, and a few politicians close to them who adamantly favor the friendship between Japan and Korea among such hardships. They might be even isolated in the political world of Japan. But they wouldn't give up, and I support them.

The Japanese government doesn't have to change its principle, but if it continues to take a too hardened attitude, it would be immature. However fiercely their opinions crash, it must not reject talks with a neighboring country; it is a folly which means giving up diplomatic efforts. Japan relies on diplomacy for its existence, thus it should recover a friendly relationship with South Korea and maintain it with a broad mind. Prime Minister Suga should accept the Japan-South Korea summit meeting; he must not reject even meetings.

Secretary-General Nikai treats and interacts with South Korea with a generous heart. I have accompanied him to South Korea several times and actually seen his interaction with important Korean persons. There is a strong human trust relationship between Nikai and some of such important persons. Therefore, I propose that Prime Minister Suga send him to South Korea as the "special envoy of the Prime Minister" to arrange the summit meeting with President Moon. We should consider it as a responsibility of the Japanese government to keep a favorable relationship between Japan and South Korea.

(2) Nikai leads the re-evaluation and resurgence of "Tanaka Kakuei politics" in LDP

Recently, a lot of books have been published which re-evaluate Tanaka Kakuei. I think it is a good and natural phenomenon. We should evaluate Tanaka, a great politician, fairly. In the 1970s, Japanese politics failed. Especially, following the U.S. establishment, which was determined to oust Tanaka, they made a big mistake of denying Tanaka politics. For Japan, this loss is unmeasurable.

In the early 1970s, a great shift occurred in the world situation.

One is that China became a superpower in the international community.

U.S. established the diplomatic relationship with People's Republic of China and recognized it as the legitimate Chinese government; U.S. ceased to recognize the Taiwanese government as the government which represented China. As a result of it, People's Republic of China became a permanent member of the United Nations Security Council. On the other hand, Republic of China in Taiwan was excluded from U.N. It was the natural course of events in the international politics.

The Japanese government also established the diplomatic relationship with People's Republic of China, and the Tanaka Cabinet which was formed on July 1972 changed the existing policy toward China fundamentally. On September, Prime Minister Tanaka and Ohira Masayoshi, the Minister of Foreign Affairs, visited China, talked with Zhou Enlai, the Premier, and Mao Zedong, the President, signed the Japan-China joint declaration and declared establishment of the diplomatic relationship between Japan and China. Asia entered a new era, and a strong bond was created which linked Japan and China.

Another is the oil crisis in 1973. Arab countries, which had been defeated again and again by Israeli forces, struck back and declared that they would not sell oil to any countries which supported Israel. The world economy, which heavily relied on oil, got into a panic.

The Japanese government deployed its own diplomatic activities and succeeded to import oil from Arab countries; the Tanaka Cabinet initiated Japan's own diplomatic activities in Middle East.

The establishment of the diplomatic relationship with China was also achieved through the diplomatic activities which the Tanaka Cabinet developed on its own. And with oil as well, it conducted its own diplomacy.

However, such diplomatic activities by the Japanese government enraged the U.S. government, and it developed a sense of distrust and caution. Then, the U.S. government cooperated with some members of the Japanese political circles who sided with it to perform the maneuver to exclude Tanaka.

Tanaka, who was called "Mr. LDP", not only fell from power but was arrested and prosecuted by the prosecutors. Furthermore, the LDP government then discarded him mercilessly. Then, Tanaka left the party voluntarily.

This was a great loss for Japan, because the outstanding ability of Tanaka Kakuei, a genius politician, ended up being used to restore his own honor, not for the Japanese people.

Forty years passed since then, but the political circles and Japanese media which have been sympathizing with the U.S. government have been cold to him, though there have been some attempts to restore his honor.

However, some attempts have been made recently to re-evaluate Tanaka Kakuei, and Nikai pushed this momentum after he became the Secretary-General of LDP. Because Nikai has told "the former Prime Minister Tanaka was my mentor" in the media repeatedly, the movement of re-evaluation of Tanaka has spread among the political circles. I have interviewed several dozen politicians of LDP recently, and not a few of them referred to Tanaka as the politician whom they respected the most. In addition, the reputation of Tanaka has been reviving not only within LDP but also in the media circles.

On October 2020, an interview "How would Mr. Kakuei think now?" by Nikai appeared in the November 2020 issue of "Monthly Japan" magazine. In this, he said as follows.

Hearing the name of "Tanaka Kakuei", one might come up with a formidable figure who makes everyone tense with his loud voice. But in fact, Mr. Tanaka was a great politician with a gentle heart.

Tanaka felt affection for people, especially for those who were in an unfortunate situation. I think it is great. We served him with respect, thinking "I can follow this person". This feeling hasn't been changed a bit even now. It has become my habit to stop and think "How would Mr. Tanaka think?" when something happens.

The Tanaka Cabinet was formed in 1972, and that year, I became a freelance writer and started interviewing in LDP to write "An Essay on LDP" which 'Chuo-Koron' asked me. It was right after Tanaka became the Prime Minister. When I visited LDP to do interviews, Hashimoto Tomisaburo, the Secretary-General, Takeshita Noboru, the head vice Secretary-General, and Okuda Keiwa, the vice chairperson of Public Relations committee cooperated with me. They were all charming and kind, and lent a hand in the interviews by a rookie freelance writer. Also, I met Tanaka Kakuei several times, including in group interviews. He was a grand and cheerful person with goodness and pure spirit. His character was quite straightforward and charming, making him a great statesman loved by everyone. As Nikai said, he was a man with a "gentle heart". Tanaka was attacked by the media for his money issue, forced to be a defendant in the Lockheed bribery scandals and leave LDP, but this was a big mistake by Japanese politicians, officials, and media persons then who colluded with the intelligence agencies of U.S.

LDP denied Tanaka Kakuei, and it was a big mistake. But the party hasn't reflected on it officially.

Nikai has begun to speak of the truth about Tanaka Kakuei and promote the re-evaluation of him. Recently, when I talked with Nikai in the office of the Secretary-General, he showed me an autograph written with a brush, saying, "I found an autograph written by the former Prime Minister Tanaka...". In it, large letters " 國魚 (the national fish)" were written. They were well-written, dynamic and unconstrained.

Nikai aims to realize "gentle politics for people", and this "gentle politics" is the same with that of Tanaka.

After the oil crises in the 1970s, the neoliberalism revolution occurred as a result of the "Thatcher revolution" by the U.K. Prime Minister Margaret Thatcher and the "Reagan revolution" by the U.S. President Ronald Reagan. It spread globally and the entire world entered an era of neoliberalism. The principle that put competition first and an idea that "anything is all right as long as they are all right themselves" pervaded the world, and economic and social disparities widened. Politics, economy, society, and even culture became cold to people and gentleness was lost from them. As a result, society deteriorated.

The Covid-19 catastrophe which began in the spring 2020 brought the biggest crisis humankind have ever faced. Within it, though, the reflection on the age of neoliberalism which has been cold to people spreads silently and deeply. More and more people realize that human society has been weakened so much because of the proliferation of the cold principle that put competition first and the individualism like "If victorious, a national army; if defeated, a band of traitors". Among the Covid-19 catastrophe, the awareness of people begins to change; societies start to change and so does politics.

I feel it is a historical necessity that a gentle politician like Nikai has become the top figure of the political world in Japan. In addition, it seems a result of the fact that people's political awareness has begun to change.

Secretary-General Nikai holds the aim that LDP practice the "gentle politics" of Tanaka Kakuei. If Nikai acts as the Secretary-General of LDP longer, it can be free from the influence of neoliberalism and develop further as a good political party which loves the common people. And when it is achieved, LDP might be able to become the true national party and realize a super long reign. How will the outcome be?

On the other hand, if LDP continues existing politics of neoliberalism, the principle that puts competition first, and the idea "anything is all right as long as they are all right themselves", the revival of Japan will be delayed. And the LDP administration then will be accused by the people for it. As a result, LDP might suffer a catastrophic loss in the next general election as in that held on August 30th 2009.

If the politics of Nikai Toshihiro, who inherited the "gentle politics" of Tanaka Kakuei, becomes the mainstream in the Japanese politics, Japan will be able to develop into the most respected country in the world. Secretary-General Nikai is the promoter of the "gentle politics" in Reiwa era.

(3) Improvement of the management of the liaison meeting between the government and ruling parties

After the "liaison meeting between the government and ruling parties" held on November 16th 2020, the statements of the Prime Minister, the leader of Komeito, and the Secretary-General of LDP were disclosed to the media. Before that, only the statements of the Prime Minister and the leader of Komeito had been disclosed.

At the previous liaison meeting, Nikai asked the members to reconsider this practice and as a result of the discussion between Kato Katsunobu, the chief Cabinet secretary, and Hayashi Motoo, the acting Secretary-General of LDP, it was decided that the statements of the Prime Minister, the leader of Komeito, and the Secretary-General of LDP would be disclosed to the media. Thus, a mistake of the former Abe Cabinet was corrected.

Though it was only natural and seemed to me an improvement, political journalists didn't accept it straightforwardly and favorably. In extreme cases, some of the media reported it in a way people would misunderstand that it was a result of Nikai exerting his influence and forcing them to include his statement. But it is not correct at all. Political journalist should be aware that they have the responsibility to convey the truth to the people.

During the period of the Abe Cabinet, the statements in the liaison meeting between the government and ruling parties which would be disclosed to the media were limited to those of the Prime Minister and the leader of Komeito. It was supposed to be strong insistence by the former Prime Minister Abe and LDP acquiesced to it.

Then the Suga Cabinet was formed, and before Suga worked out its policy, Nikai asked to improve the management of the liaison meeting and to disclose the statement of the LDP Secretary-General as well. Thanks to his proposal, a mismanagement in the period of the former Abe administration was corrected. It is a more open way toward politics to disclose the statements of the three people attending the liaison meeting.

In the sixty-five years since it was established, LDP has held power for sixty-one years. During this period, it has been complying with the principle of separation of the three branches of government: the party president, who is also the Prime Minister, is responsible for the public administration, while the Secretary-General of the party shoulder all responsibility for party management and Diet affairs. In other words, the one responsible for Diet affairs in LDP is its Secretary-General.

The leader of Liberal Democratic Party is the president (who is also the Prime Minister), and the Secretary-General holds the No.2 position. However, according to the principle of separation of the three branches of government, the Secretary-General, who is responsible for Diet affairs and party management, and the Prime Minister, who is the head of government, must be equal with regard to the relationship between the legislative and executive branches of government. Therefore, in the liaison meeting between the government and ruling parties, the Prime Minister, the Secretary-General of LDP, and the leader of Komeito have to stand on an equal footing.

In the liaison meeting, these three persons are on a par. Thus, the proposal by Nikai was quite just and appropriate for practicing parliamentary democracy.

Another point is that the trend "government takes initiative, party follows it" was too strong in the period of the former Abe administration. A system in which the government took initiative was established completely, the Diet was neutralized, and the party even seemed a subordinate organization of the government. The proper balance between the Diet, the ruling parties, and the administration had been lost.

Secretary-General Nikai has been trying to restore the balance between these three organs.

Democracy is a decentralized political system, and its principle is that the legislative, executive, and judicial branches check each other to manage politics with balance. Parliamentary democracy is a political system which centers on the Diet. It is also because the legislators who were directly elected by the people form the Diet, so it reflects the will of the people. However, under the former Abe administration, the cabinet, especially the office of the Prime Minister, monopolized power and the Diet and ruling parties were the subcontractors of it. In this sense, the actual management of the political system of Japan was distorted in the period of the former Abe administration.

This situation is not a proper image of parliamentary democracy. The political system of Japan is parliamentary cabinet system, and the highest organ of state power is the Diet. The 41st article of the Japanese Constitution clearly states, "The Diet shall be the highest organ of state power, and shall be the sole law-making organ of the State".

Though there are various theories as to what "the highest organ" means, we should understand that it was not included in the Constitution as a mere political word, but it has a legal meaning that the Diet has the supreme responsibility for the national politics in general as the highest organ under the principle of popular sovereignty. From the 41st article of the Japanese Constitution, we can see the clear intention to strengthen the position of the Diet and materialize the principle of popular sovereignty in the face of a reality that modern nations tend to center on the executive branch too much.

In this sense, the system in the period of the former Abe administration, where the cabinet took initiative too much, didn't conform to the philosophy of the Japanese Constitution.

In the actual management of politics in Japan, the office of the Prime Minister holds political power and has the decision-making authority over the personnel affairs of the high officials. And in reality, the actual political power has been wielded by the chief Cabinet secretary as well as the deputy chief Cabinet secretary, who is also the chief officer of the personnel affairs, and a few veteran officials who are close to him, in the form of exercising authority over the personnel issues. Formally, the initiative by the office of the Prime Minister seems to mean the initiative by the chief Cabinet secretary, but in reality, a few veteran officials such as the deputy chief Cabinet secretary, who are also aides of the chief Cabinet secretary, take the initiative; this is the true state of the excessive initiative by politics.

In the face of such distorted exercise of political power, we have to realize the true initiative by politics, that is, the true initiative by the Diet in the real management of the politics, which will embody the principle of popular sovereignty in the political management; we have to reverse the situation of "government takes initiative, parties follow it" and change it to "parties take initiative, government follows it". And as a first step for it, we should make it even between the government and the parties.

In the liaison meeting between the government and ruling parties, which was realized by the Nikai's initiative, the practice that only the Prime Minister and the leader of Komeito make statements before the media was changed and the Secretary-General of LDP was added to them. Though it is a small step, it should be valued highly as a first step to correct the "excessive initiative by the government and the transformation to an administrative state". From this viewpoint, I support the initiative by Secretary-General Nikai.

During the transition from the former Abe Cabinet to the Suga Cabinet, the improvement of the political management is naturally necessary. So, the proposal of Nikai about the press release of the liaison meeting should be regarded as a small but meaningful step to materialize popular sovereignty.

In order for the political system to function properly, the balance of political system distorted through the excessive initiative by the office of the Prime Minister must be restored to its normal state.

Now, the true reinstatement of the Diet is necessary.

The proper balance between the executive and legislative branches of government is especially important. Under a system in which the government takes excessive initiative, like in the period of the former Abe administration, the Diet doesn't function adequately.

Under a system of parliamentary democracy, the people express their political will and step into action through the Diet. And in the process, popular sovereignty is materialized. The members of the Diet must always listen to the voices of the people and reflect them on the national politics, but under the excessive initiative by the government, the Diet members cannot demonstrate their abilities properly. If the Diet members cannot work enough to meet the expectation of the people, the administration also will become detached from the people and lose trust from them.

We have to admit that the current politics of Japan has been detached from the people and every one of them keenly sense it. Voter turnout is decreasing and people's distrust in politics deepening. Meanwhile, the politics is leaning toward totalitarianism and an administrative state. Democracy in Japan is in crisis and such a situation must be changed.

Secretary-General Nikai faces this situation and make efforts day and night to energize the Diet. The first step for this is the disclosure of the statements by the LDP Secretary-General in the liaison meeting. However, it is just a small step; though we still have a long way to realize the politics initiated by the Diet, we have to make efforts for it.

Now is the time to restore the parliamentary democracy practically. The administration of Japan should stand on not only the cabinet but also the Diet and political parties, and the government and ruling parties have to stand on the three pillars including LDP and Komeito.

In my opinion, a society should be oval rather than concentric circle, for oval has two centers. Likewise, politics should have two centers, Diet and cabinet, and if possible, the judicial branch should become independent totally and form the third center. The government, too, should have two centers of the cabinet and the ruling party, and under the coalition administration, a system with three centers, the cabinet, LDP, and Komeito, would be better. Anyway, overconcentration is dangerous.

2. Secretary-General Nikai aims for the "diversification of Japanese diplomacy" to strengthen the diplomatic power of Japan

For many years, Secretary-General Nikai has been engaged in diplomatic activities initiated by the party or legislators in order to supplement the governmental diplomacy. And he is promoting them now, too.

Nikai looks ahead to the post-Covid 19 era and aims for the diversification of Japanese diplomacy.

Nikai is quite enthusiastic for diplomatic activities, has many friends in such countries as China, South Korea, Vietnam, and Indonesia, and has been engaged in human diplomacy. But that's not all.

Nikai is looking at the entire world. When the "World Tsunami Awareness Day (November 5th)" was established at the U.N. General Assembly, he visited the U.N. headquarters and made speech there. He has also developed diplomatic activities initiated by the party or legislators in such areas as U.S., Latin America, and Middle East.

Nikai is planning to visit U.S. as soon as possible; he is trying to establish another diplomacy, the party diplomacy, to supplement the governmental diplomacy.

The governments around the world and their leaders know well that Nikai is the kingmaker and the most powerful figure in Japan, thus they seek to meet him personally.

Diplomatic activities initiated by the party or legislators have a role not only to supplement the diplomacy between governments but to defend the national interest of Japan. They help the governmental diplomacy in solving issues which governments and their leaders cannot solve.

For example, the relationship between the Japanese and Chinese governments is not so well these days. The Japanese government and Foreign Ministry give the highest priority to the cooperation with U.S. When I surveyed recent articles of Chinese newspapers, I found that the Chinese government was keeping an eye on the movement of Suga administration; they think that Suga Cabinet is trying to form the international coalition against China with U.S., U.K., Australia, Canada, New Zealand, and so on. Thus, we have to assume that Chinese people's sentiment against Japan is getting worse.

The Chinese government reacted strongly against the summit meeting between Japan and Australia held on November 2020.

China begins to assume a firm attitude toward Australia and regulate the economic relationship with it strictly.

The Suga Cabinet thinks that even if Japan gets into alignment with Australia and assumes anti-China attitude, Chine will not assume so strict an attitude toward Japan as against Australia. But it seems too optimistic, and I cannot help but feel misgivings about it.

While Japan depends on the U.S. government for its security, it relies on China economically. If China assumes the same strict attitude toward Japan, which keeps a hostile attitude toward it, as that toward Australia, what will happen to Japanese economy and how will Japan react to it? Keeping anti-China attitude without considering these questions carefully would be too immature and dangerous.

In my opinion, Japan cannot defend its national interest so easily just by focusing on the relationship with U.S. In order to cooperate with China, diplomatic activities by Nikai will be needed.

While the U.S.-first attitude by the Foreign Ministry cannot defend

Japan, it is Nikai's human diplomacy that supplements it to defend the people and economy of Japan. His presence has been keeping the relationship between Japan and China from collapsing and fulfilling a role to maintain a stable economic relationship.

The same is true of the relationship with the Korean government. The former Abe Cabinet and Foreign Minister assumed a quite strict attitude toward South Korea. While the Korean government has been seeking to reconcile itself with the Japanese government, the attitude of Japan is still adamant even after the new Suga Cabinet was formed.

If the Japanese government clings to such an adamant attitude while South Korea is striving to improve the relationship with it, it is possible that the Korean government might turn into anti-Japan someday. Then, fierce movement against Japan will occur. It is an unfortunate situation, so the Japanese government should stop ignoring the Korean government.

However, South Korea has a ray of hope: the presence of Secretary-General Nikai Toshihiro. They know that Nikai has always said "we should get along with neighboring countries" and believe that as long as Nikai is active, the reconciliation with Japan is possible.

Now, the situation of the world is amid a great shift. How will U.S. move? How about China? How about the American Continent? How about Middle East? Depending on how U.S. will act, Japan might have a chance to become independent. Then, Japan has to survive independently, and the leading politician who equips himself with independent heart is Nikai Toshihiro.

While diplomacy has to be carried out primarily under the responsibility of the government, diplomatic activities by the Japanese government are restricted due to the relationship with U.S., and it is the diplomatic activities initiated by the party or legislators that supplement and correct them. Thus, the role of Nikai's human diplomacy is becoming greater and greater.

In carrying out diplomatic activities by the Diet members, the cooperation with the ruling parties, LDP and Komeito, is essential. I would like to ask the leadership of the two parties to make their members who are responsible for diplomacy work together. I believe it is significant that the ruling coalition parties become unified in the field of diplomacy as well.

3. The starting point of Nikai is "peace", "disaster-prevention, disaster-reduction, and national resilience", and "tourism". His endless challenge for the revival of Japan

As far as I can remember, it was mid-1980s, over thirty years ago, that I found out about an excellent politician, Nikai Toshihiro. At that time, one of the politicians with whom I met frequently was Okuda Keiwa (a member of the Lower House), a top member of the Tanaka faction. He was five years older than me and I got acquainted with him in early 1973, a year after the Tanaka Cabinet was formed. It was Hashimoto Tomisaburo, the then Secretary-General of LDP, who introduced me to him, and both Okuda and Hasimoto had been newspaper reporters before becoming politicians. They helped my reporting activities.

The one who introduced me to Secretary-General Hasimoto was Professor Yoshimura Tadashi at Waseda University and Tokai University, a famous political scholar. The one who introduced me to Professor Yoshimura was his son Tooru, then a professor at Saitama University (Philosophy) and later the president of National Graduate Institute for Policy Studies). And the one who introduced me to Professor Yoshimura Tooru was Shimizu Ikutaro, a sociologist and professor at Gakushuin University. It was at the Sunagawa Struggle in 1956 that I got acquainted with Professor Shimizu. He was one of the representative progressive intellectuals after the war and a well-known figure.

In this world, everyone is linked by human relationships; a life is the history of human relationships.

In my memory, it was at the political and economic party of Okuda Keiwa in mid-1980s that I first met with Nikai, though I had already known his name. At the moment I met with Nikai, I felt that he was a grand person and would achieve great success in the future. His kindly countenance and character, warmth, straightforwardness, cheerfulness, natural attitude, politeness, quick wit, and outstanding sensitivity—those things made me feel that he was a Tanaka Kakuei who had become reticent and a gentleman. After that, I have been paying attention to and observing him. Nikai has never tried to show off and always shown his benevolence for the people; he has been acting as a true conservative politician of common people.

Nikai and I began to have a close relationship in mid-1990s, when the Hanshin Awaji Great earthquake occurred.

Right after the earthquake, Nikai visited affected areas before any other Diet members, though he was a member of an opposition party then. His action was quick, and I was impressed by his caring for the affected people and dedicating himself to rescue activities. He also wrote a book about disaster-prevention, and I was amazed at it. Nikai is passionate at all times; especially, when some people need assistance, he has always rushed to and rescued them.

Disaster-prevention is one of the most important issues in politics and Nikai is an outstanding and leading expert on it among the Diet members.

Before that, Nikai had been engaged in promoting tourism and written a book advocating an idea of tourism-oriented country. It was another great work of him, and I read it as well. In it, he argued that in order for Japan to survive as a peaceful state, it should make efforts to promote tourism, an industry of peace. Thirty years has passed since then, and the promotion of tourism has become a central agenda of the government. Presently, the tourism industry faces difficulties due to the Covid-19 catastrophe, but we must revive it once the catastrophe come to an end.

For Nikai, orienting Japan to disaster-prevention and tourism has been his main theme as a politician. And after the Great East Japan earthquake which occurred on March 11th 2011, he has been dedicating himself to "disaster-prevention, disaster-reduction, and national resilience". As a result, "disaster-prevention, disaster-reduction, and national resilience" and "tourism-oriented country" have become the main national policies of Japan, and now Nikai is called "Mr. Resilience".

There is another point which is quite important; Nikai was engaged in diplomatic activities initiated by legislators even when he was just a member of the prefectural assembly. After he became a member of the Diet, too, he has participated in such activities enthusiastically. Okuda Keiwa, Nikai's senior fellow and ally, was also a Lower House member who was committed to diplomatic activities initiated by legislators. He focused on Asia, Africa, and Middle East countries in particular; in 1980s, when he acted as the chairperson of the diplomatic committee of the Lower House, Okuda repeatedly visited these countries and led the Japan's diplomacy with these three regions. In those days, I heard several times some Diet members of the Tanaka faction say, "Oku-chan (Okuda's nickname) went to Africa again. I wonder why he is willing to be engaged in such an unglamorous task". Despite being unglamorous, diplomatic activities initiated by legislators are costly and one cannot get political donation for it. Such activities couldn't be carried out without strong awareness of peace to ensure the eternal peace and a spirit of service for the people of developing countries. Nikai had the same ideas with Okuda and accompanied him often as a close ally; both Nikai and Okuda are enthusiastic pacifists.

Okuda didn't talk about himself much, so I couldn't hear from him in person, but an acquaintance of his told me that after graduating from the former Daiyonn (No.4) high school, he entered the Imperial Japanese Army Academy. When he was demobilized and sent home after the war, he was recommended by the principal of Daiyonn high school to go on to Kyoto University, but he aimed at Tokyo University. Though his academic performance was excellent, he failed the entrance exam and entered School of Political Science and Economics of Waseda University. He was also active as a wrestler, and after graduating from Waseda, he joined a newspaper company and became a reporter. Then, he switched to a political career. Okuda had a strong awareness of peace; I was intimate with some of Diet members of Japan Socialist Party (JSP), but Okuda's awareness of peace was just as good as that of JSP members. I have felt that Okuda treated me favorably because he knew I had been engaged in student movement and peace activities. Okuda rivaled or surpassed the excellent members of JSP as a pacifist and was a politician who had been upholding democracy.

Nikai is a hard-core pacifist as well.

Though many of leftists think that there are no pacifists among conservative politicians, it is a big mistake. Not only Nikai and Okuda, but such figures as Tanaka Kakuei, Ohira Masayoshi, Hasimoto Tomisaburo, and Esaki Masumi were also straight-out pacifists.

The starting point of Nikai as a politician is peace, disaster-prevention and national resilience, and tourism

As of 2020, peace faces a crisis. Disaster-prevention is influenced by abnormal climate and tourism is in crisis because of the Covid-19 catastrophe.

These are the issues Nikai has spent more than fifty years to cope with. In the political circles of Japan, Nikai is the leading figure of "peace diplomacy". And at the same time, he is the leading expert on the "disaster-prevention and national resilience" as well as "tourism".

Nikai is exerting his experience, wisdom, and unique "intuition" to tackle these challenges.

Nikai is planning to visit U.S. after the inauguration of the new President. I hope that Nikai meets with President Biden and the high officials, then visits China and talks with the high officials of the Chinese government including President Xi Jingping, and acts as the mediator between U.S. and China. I believe it is time for Nikai to step into action.

In 2021, Nikai faces a time of taking inventory of his life as a politician.

I believe Nikai will take action to defend peace and promote the reconciliation between U.S. and China. Furthermore, he is determined to visit North Korea. I sincerely wish Nikai to accomplish these. Nikai will dedicate his all strength to the "disaster-prevention, disaster-prevention, and national and social resilience", his greatest achievements as a politician, and be committed to the revival of "tourism", which has been greatly affected by the Covid-19 catastrophe. In addition, he will dedicate himself to the measures against the possible economic recession. And so, he will exercise his every effort to stabilize the political situation. I'm going to pay attention to the politician Nikai Toshihiro and his commitment to "getting together the collective efforts".

The biggest political issue of 2021 is the general election of the Lower House; the fate of the Suga administration depends on it. A Lower House election which is held by a new cabinet right after the former long-serving cabinet resigned tends to be difficult one, because the adverse legacy of the previous cabinet would be judged. Furthermore, the political fund-raising issue over the "eve of the gathering for cherry blossom viewing" held by the former Prime Minister Abe drives not only him but also the Suga administration into the corner. For the LDP government, the situation of the election is going to be tough. Thus, as to how to overcome this difficulty, many people place great expectations on the mastership of Secretary-General Nikai, who has been called the "genius of election".

For now, the biggest issue to be resolved is the economic recession caused by Covid-19, and the most fearful prospect thereafter is the "Covid-19 Great Depression". In order to prevent it from happening, bold economic policies are necessary. In this aspect as well, expectations on Nikai are great.

I believe Nikai has an ability and wisdom to overcome this crisis; the problem is whether the entire LDP can unite under Secretary-General Nikai. Whether LDP can gather together its collective efforts will be the biggest focus of attention.

In 2021, Japan faces a crucial moment; especially, it is imperative to resolve the two biggest issues, the Covid-19 catastrophe and economic anxiety. As well as resolving these domestic problems, it is equally important to deal with the international community properly. Nikai Toshihiro, an international politician, is looking at the world, and the "realization of eternal peace and resilience of human society" is the biggest and ultimate theme of his as a politician. Nikai will tackle these challenges with courage.

Afterword—Aiming for peace, love for home, and national
resilience as well as resilience of the global civilization

"A ruler has to look after the interests of people, not of his own" (Zhou Gong Dan)

[1]

Forgive me for my somewhat long "Afterword".

A year has passed since I finished writing my previous work, "An Essay on Secretary-General Nikai Toshihiro". The main theme of it was Nikai's way of life as a politician and I wrote it based on my experience of interacting with him for more than thirty years. My view toward him has been unchanged.

However, in writing it, I felt that Nikai became greater in his character after he had become the Secretary-General, and his aides also admit it.

Since I started to work on this book, I have interviewed some people who knew well Nikai as the Secretary-General of LDP, and they all said that he had become bigger and bigger.

As phrase goes, "He is not what he used to be". I have felt as if Nikai and I are friends because of our long-time interactions, but now I feel I must amend this attitude; I have to treat Nikai, who has become a great statesman and, furthermore, a big figure capable of creating a great history, with more respect. I also feel that someday I must apologize to him for my rudeness in the past.

The primal purpose of this book is to let people know the true image of Nikai who has become a such great politician as to be capable of moving the history of Japan.

There is a saying, "You can't see the forest for the trees". I have always been reminded of this saying when I write an essay on someone. And now, in writing an essay on Nikai, I am making efforts to understand this great forest more deeply, while being afraid that I look at only the trees in front of me, not seeing Nikai himself, a huge forest.

In order to get closer to a such great figure as Nikai, I got cooperation from those politicians who act as his aides, as well as journalists. I would like to thank them. Especially, I give heartfelt thanks to Hayashi Motoo, the acting Secretary-General of LDP, Koizumi Ryuji (a member of the Lower House), the chief of International Bureau of LDP, Tsuruho Yosuke, a member of the Upper House, Kado Hirofumi, a member of the Lower House, and Nakamura Eizo, the president of Wakayama Broadcasting System.

[2]

Here forgive me for writing my personal affairs. In the autumn of 2020, I became eighty-eight years old. Though I had been determined since my youth that I would say goodbye to this world at the age of eighty, I was healthy even after I reached this age. However, in the summer when I was eighty-two, I suffered heatstroke and was hospitalized by an ambulance. The doctor told me, "if you were discovered just one hour late, your life should have been at risk". I was released from the hospital about one month later, but soon afterward I suffered ischemic heart failure and was hospitalized again. My family was told by the doctor that I was in critical condition, but a miracle happened; I recovered from the illness just by catheterization. I was released two months later this time. After that, I was hospitalized three times with pneumonia, and they were all emergency hospitalization. I feel sorry for relying on ambulances again and again. Though I had spent five years since I became eighty-two years old hospitalized and discharged repeatedly, the medical test which I took at the end of 2019 showed that my health was improving. Thus I'm going to remain in this world for the near future; I feel somewhat sorry for this.

While I was living a stay-at-home life since early 2020 due to the Covid-19 catastrophe, I became eighty-eight years old. Everyone inevitably ceases to exist someday. Looking back my life, I am reflecting what I have not done enough to return a favor to those who helped me. However, in the face of the end of life, my mind is peaceful now; I feel that I want to follow my fate obediently.

In this process, I had a change of heart; I have become to feel as if I see all living creatures in this world from the outer world. Though my body have returned to this world, my mind hasn't returned here completely.

In the past, I lived with an awareness that I was a member of this world, but this feeling changed after illness, and I have come to see events in this world from the outside. Though I might live in this world a little longer, I will live as a phantom without regarding myself as a member of this world.

Also, my view toward politics has changed. Before my illness, I saw things in this world, including political issues, from within the society, but after my illness, I feel as if I see them from the sky.

Such psychological changes of mine affect my view toward Nikai as well. For example, in the past, I regarded him and Tanaka Kakuei as a disciple and a mentor, not as equals. But it looks different to me now; I have built an awareness that Nikai ranks with Tanaka, or he is an excellent politician who has surpassed Tanaka. While in the past I understood that he was an outstanding statesman among the current politicians, now I believe he is a historical genius.

Napoléon said, "Great men are meteors designed to burn so that earth may be lighted", and I have come to a conclusion that Nikai is a great genius of politics who has come from the heaven to brighten this dark world.

Why do I believe Nikai is a great genius of politics?

First, Nikai has a "limitless kindheartedness". Though I have met a lot of people, few politicians were as kindhearted as Nikai. Furthermore, he actually practices the saying of Zhou Gong Dan, "A ruler has to look after the interests of people, not of his own"; he perfectly practices the saying "A politician must strive for the interests of people and should not pursue his own interests".

Second, Nikai cares for his family; he respects his parents and loves his all family members. His family members also respect Nikai deeply. Most of the politicians live so tough lives as sacrificing their own family. Though Nikai also lives a life of "political activities-first", in the Nikai family there is the family head's limitless love for his family members and their deep respect for the family head. This is the result of Nikai's excellent humanity. Family is the basis of a human life, and it is an important condition for excellent politicians to have a family whose members respect and trust each other.

Third, Nikai loves his home deeply. A veteran politician with as strong an electoral base as that of Nikai would not return to his constituency every weekend, as in the period of multiple-seat constituency system. However, no matter how busy he is, Nikai frequently returns to his constituency, looks around his home, and listens to the voices of the people there. Regarding the depth of love for his home, Tanaka Kakuei and Nikai Toshihiro are on a par.

Fourth, Nikai has a limitless love for all humans; at all hours, he thinks of nothing but serving for the world and people. Thus, he is a man who is totally political in a good sense. At the same time as he loves all humankind and all the people deeply, Nikai is kind to all those whom he meets. Nikai is a genius in considering others' feelings.

Fifth, Nikai is a born leader and blessed with the ability to lead others. He can be a leader just by being among a group. Even if he just sits quietly, people accept him as their leader. Ever since he was a child, Nikai has had characteristics by which everyone accepts him as the leader.

Sixth, Nikai is always seeking the eternal peace of the world. Recently, he expressed his intention to visit North Korea to talk with the top leader directly. It is a brave statement. He showed his intention to visit the U.S. as well. Nikai is always thinking of the world peace.

Nearly forty years have passed since I became acquainted with Nikai, and he has always been the best gentleman with politeness. I have never seen him act inappropriately, nor heard that he did so. Furthermore, he never talks badly of others. To me, Nikai is a perfect, excellent, and great gentleman.

[3]

In my previous book, "An Essay on Secretary-General Nikai Toshihiro ", I mentioned the names of four persons, Katsu Kaisyu, Suzuki Kantaro, Miki Bukichi, and Nikai Toshihiro, as the great "No.2" politicians after the Meiji Restoration. And here I add one more person to the list: Kono Ichiro, a politician who accomplished the establishment of diplomatic relationship between Japan and Soviet Union, as well as Japan's admission to U.N. In other words, these five great "No.2" politicians made the Japanese history of these 150 years.

① Katsu Kaisyu, who was responsible for the bloodless surrender of Edo Castle and providing hundreds of thousands of Hatamoto samurais with means of living.

② Suzuki Kantaro, who, in the last days of World War II, restrained the army, which clung to continuing the war, and put an end to the war.

③ Miki Bukichi, who accomplished the merger of conservative parties in 1955, ten years after the war ended.

④ Kono Ichiro, who negotiated with Soviet Union in 1956, signed the Soviet–Japanese Joint Declaration, re-established the diplomatic relationship between Japan and Soviet Union, and achieved Japan's admission to U.N.

⑤ Nikai Toshihiro, who resolved the military crisis with China in 2012, which had been caused by the decision of Noda DPJ administration to nationalize Senkaku Islands ignoring the fierce opposition by the Chinese government, and built a new era of the friendship between Japan and China. In addition, he has made a lot of achievements such as the establishment of the "World Tsunami Awareness Day" and "Basic Act for Disaster-Prevention, Disaster-Reduction, and National Resilience", and making the idea of "tourism-oriented country" a national policy. And now, he is tackling a world-wide challenge of the "resilience of the global civilization", and that initiative should be praised.

Though these five figures are all "No.2" politicians, they have made greater achievements than "No.1" figures and made a history themselves.

These five "No.2" figures are hard-core pacifists. Here I say again that defending peace is the prime responsibility of politicians.

① Katsu Kaisyu not only saved the lives of the people of Edo by the bloodless surrender of Edo Castle, but blocked the plots by Britain and France to colonize Japan by taking advantage of the domestic upheavals.

② Suzuki Kantaro served as an aide of Showa Emperor, who strongly pursued peace, put an end to World War II, and opened a way to the era of peace.

③ Miki Bukichi achieved the merger of conservative parties, which had continued rivalry and conflicts for ten years during and after the war, formed Liberal Democratic Party, unified conservative forces through it, and made a base for the postwar rebuilding and economic growth.

④ Kono Ichiro achieved the establishment of the diplomatic relationship between Japan and Soviet Union, Japan's admission to U.N., and its comeback to the international community as a nation of peace.

⑤ Nikai Toshihiro reconstructed the friendly relationship between Japan and China which had been broken by the Noda DPJ administration, established a new era of the friendship between the two countries, and has made efforts to prevent the Japan-China relationship from worsening, while blocking plots by the right-wing forces to bring Japan and China into conflict. Also, he is making efforts to bring peace to the Asian region. And now, he is planning to visit North Korea to realize the peace in Asia.

These five "No.2" figures are all hard-core pacifists and has saved the peace of Japan. And Nikai is a representative politician of peace from the early Heisei Era to the early Reiwa Era.

[4]

As I wrote in my previous work, 'An Essay on Nikai Toshihiro, Secretary-General', the three greatest geniuses of the post-war politics are Miki Bukichi, Tanaka Kakuei, and Nikai Toshihiro. While I saw Miki, who was like a hermit, only once in the Diet building, I interviewed Tanaka in person several times. And I have been interacting with Nikai intimately for forty years. These three geniuses have some characteristics in common.

First, they are adept at the "art of politics". Bismarck, the political leader of Germany in 19th century, said "politics is not science, but art", and whether one equips himself with this "art of politics" decides whether he is a genius or a mediocre politician. And the "art" of these three figures is different from "Machiavellism"; it is a wisdom to realize human love.

Second, they all have unique "brainstorm", "inspiration", and "intuition". Inventor Edison said "Genius is one percent inspiration and ninety-nine percent perspiration", and it applies to the world of politics as well. While making more efforts than anyone else does, political geniuses have "inspiration", which is at the same time their unique "brainstorm" and "intuition". Both Miki and Tanaka had it, and Nikai has it too.

Third, they have an ability to read someone's mind; they are adept at mind-reading. In the past, Miki always made a friend of those who attracted his attention. It was said that Miki had some supernatural powers. A disciple of Miki repeatedly asked him about the secret of his outstanding ability to read someone's mind and make a friend of others, but he never answered to it. However, shortly before he passed away, Miki murmured in a low voice, "if you know what someone really wants, you can open up a way". I heard it from this disciple in person. Miki had an ability to read someone's mind; Tanaka had it, and Nikai has it as well.

By the way, there are two more points about these great geniuses; one is that they always look at the world, and the other is that they always look at the future.

[5]

In 2021, the world will change drastically, and the role of politics is extremely big as to how Japan should survive in this situation. I believe now is the time for experienced veteran politicians should work actively. And the leading person among such politicians is Secretary-General Nikai Toshihiro.

It seems that Prime Minister Suga is trying to tackle issues of Japan in 2021 by the force of young politicians such as Kato Katsunobu, the chief Cabinet secretary, Kono Taro, a Minister of State, Hirai Takuya, another Minister of State, Takeda Ryota, the Minister for Internal Affairs and Communications, Koizumi Shinjiro, the Minister of the Environment, and Kajiyama Hiroshi, the Minister of Economy, Trade and Industry. But it would be a miracle if the difficulties that Japan is facing now can be resolved through this lineup. Presently, the wisdom of veteran politician is necessary. Thus, if Prime Minister Suga makes light of these veteran politicians, the consequence will be dire.

In addition, Prime Minister Suga seems to depend on the promoters of neoliberalism revolution such as Takenaka Heizo. But neoliberalism is nothing more than a bad heritage from the past that had already failed. If Suga really means it, the situation will be dangerous; it is as if one repeats the same mistakes.

In order to deal with the age of drastic change after 2021, the wisdom of experienced veteran politician is essential.

Prime Minister Suga has to be humble enough to ask for advises from veteran politicians like Secretary-General Nikai.

What matters most is for all wise leaders to combine forces, that is, "gathering together their collective efforts".

When one looks back the post-war political history to this day, he will find it can be divided into a few phases.

The first phase is from 1945 to 1955. The main characteristic of this period is the three-party system of two conservative parties and Japan Socialist Party (JSP).

The second is the 1955 political system, in which LDP, the strong ruling party, and JSP were the dominant forces. It was a period of struggles between a perpetual ruling party and a perpetual opposition party.

The third is the period of two conservative parties after the single-seat constituency system was introduced. While LDP remained the same, opposition parties kept changing; such parties as New Frontier Party, The Democratic Party of Japan, The Democratic Party, Party of Hope, and The Constitutional Democratic Party of Japan (CDP) emerged and disappeared. During this period, The Democratic Party of Japan seized power once, but after three years and three months from 2009 to 2012, it suffered a crushing defeat in the Lower House election in 2012 and the LDP returned to power.

JSP, a part of the 1955 political system, was a political party based on the idea of social democracy. Social democracy is a thought which originated in the West, as with communism. Thus, any political party which believes in socialism or communism has its basis in Western thought. In progressive parties, few politicians, if any, believe in Eastern thought.

On the other hand, not a few members of conservative parties believe in it. Of course, some of them also believes in the conservatism of the West; conservative parties consist of various people.

In the mid-1970s, I spent almost three years to visit various places in Japan to survey the political awareness and ideology of ordinary people.

In rural areas, most of the members of a progressive camp were labor unionists and believers of socialism, and some were Christian socialists. Labor union, like social democracy, is a product of the Western society, and these socialists were making efforts to brainwash the Japanese people with Western thought.

By contrast, most of grassroots supporters of LDP believed in Eastern thought which had taken root in the grassroots of Japan. And majority of them were Buddhists. Furthermore, some of local leaders were believers in Confucius, as well as in Shinto or Daoism.

The Eastern thought which had taken root in Japan was based on Shinto, Buddhism, Confucianism, and Daoism. These philosophies have already blended in and lost differences. In China, Confucianism, Daoism, and Buddhism had already blended in during ancient times, and they entered in Japan to blend with Shinto as well. Originally, Buddhism and Daoism were similar, and so were Shinto and Daoism.

Now, LDP and Komeito form a coalition administration and they are getting along quite well. The electoral cooperation between them works well, too. In my view, it is because both LDP and Komeito are based on Eastern thought.

Therefore, one of the reasons why LDP and JSP continued to oppose each other and never cooperated harmoniously would be the difference in their fundamental thought.

Majority of the member of CDP, the largest opposition party now, used to be members of LDP or its sympathizers. However, though they are conservative ideologically, their conservatism is close to that of the West. Politicians like Ozawa Ichiro, who was committed to introducing the single-seat constituency system, adored the politics of the U.K. and U.S. Also, many of the promoters of neoliberalism are those politicians who adore the U.S. so much.

JSP, a part of the post-war 1955 political system, has ceased to exist in effect, and one of the reasons is that the socialism as a Western thought couldn't be accepted by the Japanese people.

The coalition administration of LDP and Komeito is stable because these parties are based on Eastern thought (LDP on various Eastern philosophies, Komeito on the Lotus Sutra, the Buddhism preached by Nichiren).

If CDP wants to have a strong base among the Japanese people, it should understand Eastern thought. Unless it lets go of its lukewarm character, CDP might be far from seizing power unless the coalition administration of LDP and Komeito makes some big mistakes or collapses.

In Wakayama, the birthplace of Nikai, there are Kumano Kodo (old road) and Kumano Shrine, both a holy place of Shinto. Also, there is Kohya mountain, the holy place of Buddism. Kii Peninsula faces the Pacific Ocean, so various cultures, religions, and philosophies of Asian countries entered there and blend together in the land of Wakayama. Nikai is deeply familiar with these cultures, religions, and philosophies, so he can be called "Mr. Wakayama".

Present political challenges Nikai faces now involve a lot of important issues: to overcome the Covid-19 catastrophe, to take a role for normalizing the relationship between the U.S. and China, to establish peace in Asia, to dialogue with North Korea to resolve the abduction issue, to stabilize the lives of the Japanese people and the economy of Japan, to make Japan highly ethical, to realize disaster-prevention, disaster-reduction, and national resilience, to develop tourism-related enterprises, and to eradicate unemployment.

Among them, the huge issue of the reconciliation between the West and the East might not be resolved without Nikai. I sincerely hope that he will tackle this historical task.

While one of the biggest achievements of Nikai is placing the "national resilience" at the center of Japanese politics, we have to work on not only the resilience of hardware but that of software as well. I call it the "resilience of global civilization" and regard it as a new challenge for Nikai.

As I repeated in this book, the ultimate political goal of Nikai Toshihiro, a genius politician with deep love for his home, international perspective, and the future-oriented ideas, is to "realize eternal peace and the resilience of the global civilization". The ultimate purpose of politics is to establish the human society which is peaceful, strong, flexible, and kind-hearted. Thus, I hope to see vigorous efforts of Nikai.

While I was writing this book, a lot of people lent a helping hand to me.

I give thanks to everyone who kindly cooperated with my interviews, everyone who took on the tasks of editing and organizing my manuscripts, and the staffs of Ronso-sya, which published this book following my previous works 'An Essay on Nikai Toshihiro, Secretary-General' and "The Challenge of Shisui-kai".

As a conclusion, I hope that Nikai Toshihiro, a genius politician, lives longer than his great mother Mrs. Nikai Kikue and exert himself at least for the next ten years, for the sake of the eternal peace of the world, the resilience of the global civilization, all humanity, and the people of Japan.

May 2021

Morita Minoru

Morita Minoru was born in 1932 in Ito, Shizuoka Prefecture. He graduated from the University of Tokyo's Engineering Department and, after holding such positions as the chief of publication department of Nihon Hyoron-Sya and the editor-in-chief of "Economic Seminar" magazine, got established as a political commentator in 1973. After that, he has been active in various areas such as radio, publication, and lectures. He is an honorary professor of Shandong University, a visiting professor of Higashi Nippon International University, and the director of "Morita Minoru Research Institute for the Global Civilization".

He has published many works, including '森田実の言わねばならぬ 名言123選', '一期一縁', '公共事業必要論', '防災・減災に資する 国土強靱化政策が日本を救う！', '森田実の永田町政治に喝！'. And he posts his essays on Facebook occasionally.

The New Challenge of Secretary-General Nikai Toshihiro

First edition: 10 September 2021

Author: Morita Minoru

Publisher: Ronso-sha Co., Ltd.

Kitai Building 2F, 2-23, Kanda Jinbo-cho, Chiyoda-ku, Tokyo.

Tel: 03 (3264) 5254   Fax: 03 (3264) 5232

Designer: Munetoshi Jyun-ichi

Printing and Binding: Chuo-Seihan-Insatsu Co., Ltd.   Typesetting: Flex Art

ISBN 978-4-8460-2088-0   Copyright ©Morita Minoru, 2021   printed in Japan

二階俊博の新たな挑戦

森田実 著／2021 年 6 月刊行
1091 円＋税／四六判上製
ISBN 978-4-8460-2062-0

多角的な証言に支えられて、二階政治の原点は〈平和主義〉と〈郷土愛〉と喝破。平和・博愛・忠恕の政治家＝二階俊博は、コロナ危機を克服し、人類が安心して生活できる安全な社会を築くために、限りなき挑戦を続けているとする。

二階俊博幹事長論

ナンバー1を越えたナンバー2実力者／平和・博愛・忠恕の政治家

森田実 著／2020 年 4 月刊行
1091 円＋税／四六判上製
ISBN 978-4-8460-1937-2

斬新な視点で描く、二階俊博の全体像。歴史は「ナンバー1ではなく、ナンバー2実力者を軸にして動く」とする著者が、《南方熊楠の和歌山魂と自由精神の継承者》である二階俊博の政治的業績を多角的に検証する。